THE PROMISE

THE PROMISE

How an Everyday Hero Made the Impossible Possible

ARNOLD DIX

SIMON & SCHUSTER

New York · Amsterdam/Antwerp · London · Toronto · Sydney · New Delhi

THE PROMISE
First published in Australia in 2025 by
Simon & Schuster (Australia) Pty Limited
Level 4, 32 York Street, Sydney, NSW 2000

10 9 8 7 6 5 4 3 2 1

New York Amsterdam/Antwerp London Toronto Sydney New Delhi
Visit our website at www.simonandschuster.com.au

A catalogue record for this book is available from the National Library of Australia

ISBN: 9781761429170

Cover design: Luke Causby/Blue Cork
Front cover photography: Arnold Dix
Back cover photography: Arnold Dix
All photos, unless otherwise stated, supplied by Arnold Dix
Typeset by Midland Typesetters, Australia
Printed and bound in India by Replika Press Pvt. Ltd.

The paper this book is printed on is certified against the Forest Stewardship Council® Standards. Griffin Press holds chain of custody certification SCS-COC-001185. FSC® promotes environmentally responsible, socially beneficial and economically viable management of the world's forests.

NOTE TO READER:
Some of the names and descriptions in this book have been changed to protect identities.

As we delve into the earth's depths, may we uncover
wisdom and strength, for in the hidden chambers
lie the secrets of life and prosperity.
Atharva Veda

CONTENTS

PROLOGUE

You really should not know who I am.

The name 'Arnold Dix' should mean nothing to most people, given that I have spent the past few decades of my professional life existing largely in the shadows. That is how the organisations I have worked for tended to like it, and it is how I preferred things, too.

Come in, get the job done and go home again. No fanfare. Minimal fuss. Everyone is happy.

In late 2023, everything changed. My approach – my entire life, if I am being honest – was completely upended by a single catastrophic event on the other side of the world. There was no going back.

Arnold Dix had to emerge into the light.

The scale of the situation and the bizarre set of coincidences that saw me wind up in a remote part of India, high in the Himalayas, trying to make the impossible a reality, demanded that I no longer be anonymous.

In November that year, forty-one young men had become trapped inside a section of a tunnel that was under construction, and it was a race against the clock to get them out safely.

When a call came, asking me to help, I felt like it was meant to be. Before I even got to that faraway mountain, I was filled with an unusual sense of purpose. I had a duty to fulfil. I was compelled by something unfamiliar inside of myself to step up and do whatever needed to be done.

And weirdly, in hindsight, it would become clear that I had been preparing for that monumental mission for months. Long before the tunnel collapsed. Without even knowing it.

For reasons I still do not quite understand, and which are fairly uncomfortable for me to ponder, I took a series of inexplicable steps that put me on a collision course with one of the most significant underground rescue attempts in modern human history.

Without knowing it, and seemingly by total coincidence – multiple coincidences – I was in the right place at the right time to help achieve something that has never really been done before.

Now, here we are. The nameless and faceless man who I used to be is gone, and in his place is a guy described in lofty terms by the leader of this great country of ours.

The Honourable Anthony Albanese, Prime Minister of Australia, delivering a statement by indulgence in the House of Representatives on 29 November 2023:

Mr Speaker, I rise to acknowledge a truly great Australian, Professor Arnold Dix, for what he has done in once again improving relations between Australia and our great friends in India.

Today, because of him and his hard work alongside the Indian authorities, forty-one people are alive, safe and free. This is an extraordinary story.

For over two weeks, the world has been gripped by these forty-one construction workers trapped in a collapsed mountain tunnel in northern India. As we know only too well, that's the sort of story that often ends in tragedy.

But this didn't, and that's where Professor Dix comes in. He's the president of the International Tunnelling and Underground Space Association, and he is an expert in these sorts of matters. It was a painstaking process, tackling a disaster like none he had ever seen.

Professor Dix put it this way: '. . . if we make a wrong move, everyone dies. Not only does everyone die who is in there but probably us as well.'

His wife sent him a message saying she didn't want him to go in, but, of course, he did. If people have seen some of his accounts, it's quite extraordinary what he did to help people who he's never met.

He and his team have succeeded. These forty-one lives have been saved, families have been reunited and our friends in India are quite rightly rejoicing.

To Prime Minister Narendra Modi, I say I'm very pleased that an Australian was able to come to India's aid at this time.

Professor Dix summed it up best when he said, 'It's about helping your friends.' Two nations, Australia and India, are now in his debt. This great Australian, with his cool head, his big heart and his expertise in a very narrow area, I've got to say – I doubt whether anyone in this chamber knew that the International Tunnelling and Underground Space Association was a thing, but it is – is amazing. I pay tribute to him on behalf of, I think, everyone here in the parliament today.

When I heard that Prime Minister Anthony Albanese had stood in Parliament to deliver some heartfelt remarks about me and my role in the rescue, I could not quite believe it. I was sure that I must have died, had a psychedelic-style reaction to the wrong kind of mushroom in a risotto and become delusional, or perhaps slipped into a dream-filled coma after a massive stroke.

How often does a prime minister have reason to say something nice about an engineer? How often is a bloke like me described as 'a truly great Australian'?

The plaudits continued on the other side of the political aisle in parliament, with Opposition Leader Peter Dutton joining his arch rival to thank me. It seemed that humble Arnold Dix had provided some common ideological ground for a brief moment in time.

Now *that* sounds truly delusional.

Up until this point, not many people outside of my immediate circles knew what I did for work, thanks to my long list of qualifications and professional pursuits. Some of which are fairly unexpected, to say the least.

For instance, I have lived in the rural community of Monbulk, Victoria, about an hour from Melbourne, for the better part of thirty years. Before the rescue, before my face was suddenly on the evening news and in newspapers, they assumed that I somehow sustained myself and my family by being a very ordinary flower farmer.

I grow sunflowers. Very unsuccessfully. I'm probably the least accomplished flower farmer in the whole state. But I like them. If we have a good crop, fantastic. If not? That's OK, too.

As my mum taught me when I was a boy – do whatever you want, but just give it a good crack. Those values, the work ethic she instilled in me, is perhaps why I have given so many things a crack.

To many others I have encountered in life, I am a lawyer and barrister, working in top-tier law firms on technical–scientific environmental cases and regularly making a nuisance of myself in the traditional and old-fashioned world of law.

Among an entirely different group of people, I am a scientist and geologist, who spends a lot of time underground, sometimes doing things that I am unable to talk about because they are highly confidential and other times dealing with death and destruction on a scale that no ordinary, innocent person should have to see in their lifetime.

The odd thing is that most people I encounter cannot see my many hats. They only recognise the Arnold they know. Just the lawyer. Just the scientist. Just the guy who delivered some plants during the Covid lockdowns. I am essentially hidden in plain view. So varied are those hats in style, colour and vintage, so absurd are some of them, that I can switch one out for another, or don several at a time, and nobody really seems to notice.

After I got home from India, one of my trucking mates phoned me up, his voice dripping with amazement down the line.

'There's a guy on TV talking about tunnels and he looks just like you,' he laughed. 'You wouldn't believe it. I think they said his name is Arnold, too. What are the chances?'

Slim, I would say.

I am a volunteer university professor, the elected president and head of an international Geneva-based association of experts that boasts about 150,000 members from eighty-one different countries, and an expert who speaks regularly at conferences and seminars across the world.

For a small number of people, I was briefly a trainee hairdresser, an apprentice welder, a contract pest and vermin controller, and a truck driver for a local nursery.

At various points in my life, I have been described as an enigma. I have been called chaotic and a little bit nuts. Some call me a nerd. Someone once said I was the embodiment of one big, never-ending midlife crisis, such is my tendency to pick up a new hobby – or a new career – and run hard with it.

I do not see it that way. I see these different skills I have collected over the decades as being useful tools that are constantly at my disposal. And they are utensils that I can whip out to assist someone in need.

Tell me your problem, and I will see if I can help solve it.

Some of those tools are a bit sharper and more reliable than others. Take welding. If there are 100 welders in all of Victoria, I am going to be the 101st best welder out there. But I will have a go.

The varying qualifications I have picked up might prove useful one day. They might come in handy if ever I am called upon to assist. Like in the rescue of forty-one men inside a collapsed tunnel in India.

Understandably, having been so many different things in my life probably does give plenty of people the impression that I am just a bit eccentric.

And I am, to be fair. I think that much is obvious, but if not, come and check out the shed on my farm. It's full of eighteenth-century pump organs that I have rescued off Facebook Marketplace and from second-hand stores.

I have about forty of them, at least, which I am restoring one by one. I have no idea why. I just like the idea of taking something that has no real value or purpose these days – seriously, you can get one for free because no-one wants them – and breathing new life into it. Imagine if they could sing. Or better yet, imagine if they could tell the stories of lives long spent and replay songs from Australia hundreds of years ago.

I am still getting used to a new label that has been attached to me – hero. I do not see myself as a hero, though. Not even close. I am simply a guy who had a few skills, who knew a couple of things, and felt like he could help in a difficult situation.

In reality, I am a pretty normal guy. My only superpowers are the ability to remain calm and think clearly, and an overwhelming motivation to be kind.

But that experience in India at the end of 2023, being able to play a role in saving the lives of forty-one men, whose fate seemed to be sealed, makes for a great story. So too do the months leading up to it, which are bizarre and mysterious. And there are some intriguing threads from throughout my life that are woven into the Indian tunnel rescue, too.

So here I am, writing a book about the experience, about my experiences, and about the things that the rescue has taught me.

If you are hoping for a boys' own adventure–style book with heart-racing action, daredevil antics and plenty of clichéd descriptions of a great guy built of different stuff needing to come in and save the day . . . this is not that book.

Instead, I would like it to be a book that enables other people to listen to themselves and trust that they know what the right thing to do is. I believe that if we take the time to listen to ourselves, to reflect, we will figure out what is right.

We live in an age of noise, where fear of failure justifies the great doing of nothing. Where the power of goodness, the idea that collectively and united we can achieve great things, is crushed by the retelling of ever-louder stories of all the evil deeds of a few.

My career has focused on the importance of life. I have devoted half of my life to rescue, recovery and protection of human life with a laser focus. And yet, I am not a perfect example of morality. I am no angel. Aggressive attempts to kill me, carried out by bloodthirsty men in a far-off tunnelling land, taught me that I too could kill, in the name of self-defence, if needed.

But when given the chance to exact a violent revenge, I realised that the intentional killing of people only leads to more killing. Even soldiers, with the exception of a few recent infamous examples, only kill to protect their mates – not killing for killing's sake.

If this book helps people on their own journeys to understand themselves, that is three-quarters of 21st-century civilisation emerging right there. You are not at the whim of social media or mass media. You can trust yourself a bit.

I think a lot of good could come from being in that frame of mind.

Of course, don't worry, what happened in India – from the collapse to the nerve-wracking rescue operation, and of course the miraculous outcome that defied all conventional wisdom – is definitely detailed in the pages to follow.

In that respect, there is plenty to dive into. And we will. Especially why I made an extraordinary promise before even arriving at the site – a promise I would probably not have made in any other scenario but which, in the moment, felt absolutely right.

The real story of how I came to be in India, of how I played a part in something truly epic, begins long, long before late 2023.

It is an almost unbelievable course that I charted from the time I was a kid, with the help of a box of rocks I found in a dead guy's room in my family's hotel, a bunch of weird men who led me into a hole in the ground, and the design for an improvised explosive device.

CHAPTER ONE

WORST POSSIBLE WORST-CASE SCENARIO

It was half-past five on the morning of 12 November when a major collapse occurred about 250 metres inside the entrance to the under-construction Silkyara Bend–Barkot tunnel project, in the Himalayas in a remote part of India.

Half a world away, preparing to sit down for lunch with a few colleagues at a conference in New Zealand, I could not possibly predict just how life-changing this event was to be. For the men trapped during the collapse, for countless rescue workers who would toil tirelessly around the clock to reach them, and for me.

In the months leading up to that fateful morning, work had proceeded at pace on digging the tunnel, which was to form part of an ambitious highway initiative to connect four holy Hindu pilgrimage spots in the far northern state of Uttarakhand.

Building a tunnel is a challenge in the best of situations. It requires careful engineering, to say the least, as well as a heavy dose of patience and a healthy budget. But in this scenario, the arduous environmental conditions that the hundreds of workers were navigating each day added an extra layer of complexity.

I cannot think of a more challenging part of the world in which to try and build a tunnel.

The mountainous state of Uttarakhand is home to several soaring, jagged Himalayan peaks and spectacular, ancient glaciers. It is incredibly remote, it is bitterly cold in the winter months, and it can be utterly unforgiving.

In fact, 'unforgiving' is too kind a description. The sheer beauty of the Himalayas masks the stark truth, that given the chance – and without warning – the mountains will try to kill you. And it won't take much.

It is also here that you will find some of the holiest sites in the world for Hindu people.

Each year, countless Hindus traverse the Chota Char Dham pilgrimage circuit to pray, make offerings and give thanks. The visitors take in one or all four sites – Gangotri, Yamunotri, Kedarnath and Badrinath.

These special spiritual destinations are broadly in the same region, close to each other, at least in the context of a country as vast as India. However, getting around is not as simple as jumping in a car and hitting the paved open road, arriving comfortably and safely at your destination a little while later.

The paths taken by so many faithful are narrow and

winding. You will not find sealed, bitumen roads here. Goat tracks are more the norm.

Gangotri is about ninety kilometres from the town of Uttarkashi, which is the main hub of Uttarakhand. Here, visitors will find the origin of the sacred Ganges River, the Bhagirathi River, which is fed by the spectacular Gangotri glacier. It is considered to be the home of the Hindu goddess Ganga. Ganga is the personification of the Ganges River, and symbolises purification and forgiveness.

Not far from the Bhagirathi River, you will find a stone where it is said King Bhagiratha offered a holy penance to the god Shiva, known as the Great God and one of the principal deities of Hinduism. Offerings are made to Shiva to bring the goddess Ganga down from the heavens to earth, to free people from their sins. Hindus believe that when Shiva let down his glorious, luscious locks of hair, the river was born.

Sitting among the Himalayas, ancient glaciers and dense forest is Gangotri Temple. This brilliant white structure was built in the nineteenth century in honour of Ganga. You only need to see images of it to understand why so many flock here. It's a real beauty.

Yamunotri is about 150 kilometres from Uttarkashi. It is the source of the Yamuna River, sitting in the shadow of the Champasar Glacier on Kalind Mountain. Venturing to the enormous glacier itself, and the frozen lake that surrounds it, is not possible for most pilgrims, given how treacherous the journey is about a kilometre further up Kalind Mountain. So the holy shrine of Yamunotri, devoted to the goddess Yamuna, was built at the foot of the hill.

Then there is Kedarnath Temple, some 240-odd kilometres from Uttarkashi, which is one of twelve sites devoted to Shiva and arguably the most challenging to visit. To reach it, pilgrims must set off on a 22-kilometre trek up a steep incline. The area is prone to extreme weather, meaning the holy site is closed during winter from December to March. During that time, the entire temple structure is carefully carried down the hill to the town of Ukhimath, so worship can continue during the blisteringly cold months.

Finally, Badrinath is home to a temple built in honour of the god Vishnu. The area is another one that is regularly impacted by severe weather conditions, so it too is only open for half the year, from late April to early November.

Getting to these four holy sites has always been a long and risky mission. The few roads and paths that exist between pilgrimage spots are treacherous. Those travelling along them are regularly greeted with the chilling site of car, bus and truck wreckages littered throughout the deep, overgrown valleys far below. They serve as a tragic reminder of just how much is at stake.

Just a month before the tunnel collapse, a bus carrying a load of pilgrims was involved in a horrible accident that killed thirty-nine people.

Those embarking on this spiritual journey are also forced to traverse parts of it by foot, taking in gruelling mountain ranges and navigating dense and confusing forest.

Hence, the construction of a highway – and the Silkyara Bend–Barkot tunnel – would make it easier and safer for worshippers to get around.

While linking holy sites is an important task in itself, constructing this highway and tunnel is part of a broader nation-building agenda set by state and national governments. Billions of dollars are being spent on infrastructure initiatives right across India to provide employment, stimulate economic growth, and better service cities and towns in far-flung parts of the country.

To the agitators, these tunnels are seen as a way to boost India's military access to its remote Himalayan borders. But, in my view, that's not their primary purpose. Sure, military vehicles could drive through them, but let's not forget – soldiers need to pray too.

Among these works are about thirty tunnels of varying lengths dotted right across the enormous landmass, with some at extraordinary heights above sea level. The conditions faced by those embarking on these feats of engineering greatness are also diverse, although all present their own challenges – some of which have not been anticipated.

Unfortunately, the area where the Silkyara Bend–Barkot tunnel was being built is a hotbed of natural disasters. It endures just about everything Mother Nature can possibly throw at it – floods, cloudbursts, avalanches, landslides, mudflows and earthquakes.

These major events have regularly caused significant damage to villages and a devastating loss of life.

This part of the world is extremely geologically active, so tunnelling in areas like Uttarkashi is risky business. These sites are especially vulnerable to landslides, which is what went wrong in this particular instance.

In an instant, a group of workers became trapped behind an unimaginably huge pile of debris inside a dark, damp tunnel. A landslide, contained entirely within a mountain, left behind a cavernous void with a 40-metre-high and 100-metre-wide hole inside the mountain. And it was growing, minute by minute, hour by hour, often in small increments but sometimes with sharp ferocity, as the earth kept rumbling in fury.

A rescue operation was quickly launched but, initially, hope of finding survivors was low. Put simply, when a tunnel caves in, it is usually a case of retrieving bodies, not finding workers who are somehow still alive.

This was not one of those situations, it quickly emerged.

All those stuck on the other side of a thick wall of rock had survived. But one small misstep, one single error made in the efforts to reach them, and all forty-one men trapped would die. Those working frantically to free them would probably be killed, too.

Tunnelling would have to be one of the riskiest occupations out there. Among all those dangerous jobs, working underground – the act of brutally piercing the earth then bravely delving into it – must surely rank pretty highly on the scary scale.

Those who choose to take on this kind of work tend to be fully aware of just how high the stakes are. How could you not? You sign up to go where few humans have ever gone. You do not need to be well-versed in geology or engineering to be acutely aware of how unwelcome us mere mortals are in these spaces.

Disasters underground are not tragedies that happen in far-off places without sophisticated technology or knowledge. Do not be fooled. Accidents and catastrophes take place everywhere. There is always a tension between humans and the earth wanting to close up whatever hole we have made, and it happens here in Australia.

In March 2024, a catastrophic rockfall inside a gold mine in Ballarat took the life of a young man and critically injured another. An investigation is underway to determine what went wrong and whether it could have been prevented.

Just before the collapse, the men were part of a team doing something called air-legging. Air-legging involves a hand-held drill with a compressed air–driven hammer that smashes through the rock it meets. It can be a risky practice because it requires you to be so close to the rock. If something goes wrong, as it did in this case, the person is right where the rockfall happens.

What role the practice played in this particular instance is still unclear. The brutal fact is that there is always a risk involved in working underground. You do not know what you are dealing with until you find yourself smack bang in the middle of it.

In August 2024, three tunnel workers were trapped inside a collapsed train tunnel in Pak Chong district in northeastern Thailand, about 200 kilometres from the capital Bangkok. For the first few days they were alive and well – but when rescue workers finally got to them – after three days of being trapped – they were found dead due to lack of air.

In India, as is the case in most countries, going underground is a matter of life and death too. Regardless of the type of project, the vast majority of the men – and some women – who take on these jobs begin each day knowing that it could be their last. They accept their fate, which hinges entirely on the fragile deal struck between excavation engineers and the whim of the mountain.

Or in the case of Hindus, at the whim of gods and goddesses whose actions are unpredictable and unquestioned.

About 1000 kilometres further north of the Silkyara Bend–Barkot tunnel project, even deeper into the Himalayas, work is currently progressing on the Zojila tunnel. It will be a beast when work wraps up in 2030. It's almost ten metres wide, about seven-and-a-half metres tall, and more than fourteen kilometres long, making it the largest tunnel in Asia. It will form part of the Srinagar-Kargil-Leh National Highway.

What makes the job of tunnellers on this project even more perilous is the fact that it sits at more than 3500 metres above sea level. The scale, complexity and gruelling environment are why the whole thing is estimated to cost about US$1 billion.

When complete, it will slash the time it takes to travel the Zojila pass from at least four hours to just fifteen minutes. Zojila will offer safe and all-weather passage between the Kashmir Valley and Ladakh region. It is a mammoth nation-building endeavour – and also one of military significance, given it sits quite close to India's borders with China and Pakistan.

But the whole thing is behind schedule. The conditions workers have encountered, including some pretty severe weather, have seen the completion date pushed back several times now. At the time of writing, it was expected to open to the public at the end of 2030. We shall see. The environment here is clearly challenging for the engineers.

A recent documentary about the project heard from several of the men helping to bring the ambitious idea to life. As one bluntly but truthfully put it: 'Death is in God's hands. It can happen inside or outside the tunnel.'

In other words, everyone who ventures into that particular tunnel, or any tunnel really, during its construction is startlingly aware of just how much could go wrong and just how devastating the consequences could be.

When you are building a tunnel, you cannot simply take the equivalent of an enormous round drill bit and start cutting. Once you have penetrated a mountain, the top and sides of the tunnel structure are subjected to extreme force. I struggle to find the words to describe just how intense that pressure is. Imagine trying to get an elephant to stand on an egg without cracking it. It is possible but difficult. I reckon I saw that trick at a circus when I was kid. But it is very, very easy to get it wrong. When you do, you wind up with a big mess.

Everything above and on either side of that sudden new void is pushing inwards, quite naturally, in a bid to refill the hole you have just dug. The job of engineers is to figure out how to fool the mountain by distributing the load around the new hole. A tunnel will collapse if your deception is not finely tuned. We cannot hold up mountains. It is as simple as that.

For all the brilliant technological advances humans have made in history, we still have not quite figured out how to always support a mountain when we burrow through it. Not perfectly, anyway.

In a sense, tunnellers have to trick the mountain by using complex physics. We have to work out how to precisely distribute the crushing load of the mountain around the tunnel in such a way that it does not cave in.

Make no mistake. Modern tunnelling can be done very safely, as it is across the world every single day. Please do not find yourself terrified to drive through one on your way to and from work. Safe tunnelling is one of the greatest achievements of the twentieth century.

When you enter the remnants of a tunnel after something dire has taken place, like a collapse or landslide, you might notice something quite stark. What should be a perfect semi-circle or semi-oval depending on its size – the sign of perfectly distributed pressure – now looks like someone has taken to it with a crowbar. You will notice the top is sagging and the sides are warped. We call this 'convergence'. It describes the tunnel naturally healing itself.

Convergence is a sure sign that the mountain is about to completely reclaim the piece of itself that humans have clawed away. It has not been tricked. The mountain has cottoned on to what humans are trying to do and it is pretty pissed off about it.

This is exactly what I saw the first time I went inside the Silkyara Bend–Barkot tunnel. That particular mountain was about as angry as I have ever seen in my three-decade-plus career working underground.

When the tunnel collapsed, I was in Auckland presenting at a conference. It just so happened to be the first day of Diwali, the Hindu festival of lights.

Celebrated over several days, Diwali marks a spiritual victory of light over darkness, knowledge over ignorance, and good over evil. In the most sacred area of the Himalayas, right where this tunnel was being built, Diwali also signifies an awakening of the sleeping gods.

And so you can imagine the significance of such a devastating event taking place on the third and most holy day of Diwali.

As the elected president of the International Tunnelling and Underground Space Association, the world's largest underground industry group, I was notified of the collapse within hours. I sent out an unofficial alert to the key technical members I trusted the most and began assembling an unofficial team of specialists who could be called on if and when needed. Experts from across the globe began sharing knowledge and advice with me, which I relayed to the Indian specialists, who were both onsite and working from afar, preparing a response. My call was not official – it was personal. We of the underground are like a global tribe – we help each other – we need to.

The chief engineer of the National Highways Authority of India, Rahul Gupta, called me on the day of the collapse. I had met him a couple of times in 2023 – once in Spain and once in India. He is the epitome of an honourable man. A brilliant mind and kind soul, he is totally committed to the betterment of his country and his people.

When I heard about the collapse, as well as worrying about those inside at the time, my mind also ventured to Rahul and the enormity of the task he and his team were facing.

When we spoke, it was still very early in the rescue, so no-one was really sure if anyone had been killed during the initial disaster, or whether people were trapped, dead or alive, beneath the rockfall itself.

At that stage, the landscape was still moving. Bits and pieces of the tunnel ceiling were breaking off and plunging to the ground pretty frequently for several hours afterwards. When I heard this, my heart sank. That was not a good sign.

Rahul told me he was going to jump in a helicopter and head up there to have a look for himself. It was simply too difficult to know how bad things were and what kind of response was needed without seeing the disaster up close. After that, Rahul said he would phone me back with more specific information and see if I had any thoughts to share.

By Day Two of the rescue, a 120-millimetre pipe – that's just twelve centimetres, or the width of a CD – was successfully converted from a pneumatic air pipe for tools to a crude air, water, food, communications and medical supply line.

This makeshift connection between rescue workers and those stuck allowed for the flow of life. Tiny packets of essentials were shot from one side to the other with compressed air.

Remember those antiquated but effective tube transportation systems that offices and banks had in the old days? You know, the systems where you could pop some paperwork in a container, place it into an opening in the wall, and it would be sucked through an intricate network of pipes to its recipient? Picture that, but much smaller and operating through a pile of rock and dirt, high in the Himalayas.

The pipe, which moments earlier had been attached to a piece of industrial equipment, still had the oily frothy remnants of an old compressor within it. But it was a lifeline. The mountain was letting us deliver what we needed to keep those men alive – food, water, air and medicine. Just.

This modest but crucial pipe also allowed rescuers to communicate with the trapped workers. Miraculously, it seemed that no-one had been injured in the initial collapse. The men were alive and well – or what you might call 'well-ish' – against all odds and most expectations. There was hope where usually there is none.

Work began on a larger pipe-jacking exercise to create a small tunnel through the rubble, via which the men could escape. But even from Auckland, I could sense that this would be a challenge. The thousands of tonnes of avalanche debris was extremely unstable, I was told, so digging would need to be slow and careful.

The risk of triggering another landslide was high. Not only could the workers be injured or die, but those working to free them might very well meet a similar fate.

Usually, these types of disasters do not end well. Only in very few instances is there reason to be hopeful. Most of those involved in a collapse do not survive. I have seen the deadly aftermath of a tunnel failure plenty of times in my career.

I cannot think of a single instance in which I have been involved where there hasn't been a fatality, or several. I had never rescued anyone alive before. For decades, my work has involved seeking lessons from the dead.

Let me be blunt. On the occasions when I have been called upon to assist with the response to a collapse or investigate its cause, even when I have done so from afar, the mission always ends up being about the recovery of bodies. Not live people. It's always about finding those who have perished, clearing a path for work to eventually resume and trying to find lessons to learn.

What has always struck me is just how small the site of death appears when you see it up close with your own eyes. It is usually a little hole in the roof of a tunnel, from which a pile of stuff has fallen onto people below.

In one particularly bad case I worked on, a relatively modest piece of rock debris measuring maybe three square metres and barely 100 millimetres thick was responsible for robbing the planet of four souls. Among that thin pile of rocks and dirt were four hardhats, holding nothing but lights, ranks and names. That's all.

An event so tragic, so unspeakably shattering for those four loving circles of many families and friends, came about from something that appeared so insignificant to the naked eye.

On Day Three of the rescue, my phone rang again. It was Rahul. Since we had last spoken, I had boarded a flight from New Zealand to Germany, before moving on to Slovenia. He gave me an update on the situation.

At the rescue site, a team had attempted to drill an 800-millimetre-diameter tunnel through the debris, he explained. That was as big as they could reasonably dig. Getting a larger-diameter pipe jack up to the top of the mountain in time would not be possible. So they made the best with what they had.

The machine they were using is called a pipe jack with an incorporated auger. An auger is a bit like a huge sausage mincer that breaks up the rock it meets. As it tore through a mixture of soft ground and boulders, it encountered huge bits of torn metal, buried equipment and chunks of cement that had plunged from the collapsing roof. It kept getting stuck and Rahul was concerned the plan was destined to fail.

He asked me what I thought. I called upon the team of international experts I had already assembled to assess the situation and share any ideas we might have. We put together a rough proposal for a rescue that we would run if we were there, including the design of an alternative technique that could be implemented. It was all very informal but we at least had the rough outline of an idea, in case it was needed.

In tandem, the Indian team was trying to find a bigger auger that could feasibly be airlifted to the site. The thinking – and hope – was that a more powerful machine could beat the seemingly immovable mess concealed within the debris. Rahul asked me if I thought there was a chance of success.

I did not; I was worried it was the wrong tool for this job. But I would do everything I could to support the team. You see, I do not treat my own opinions as anything more than a single person's view. It is honestly held, but it comes from my narrow perspective.

I am a problem-solver, not a loud-mouthed know-it-all. Opinions shared should never be solutions dictated. Not when so is much at stake and every voice is worth hearing.

My philosophy when it comes to these sorts of things is that it does not really matter if something is right or not when all is said and done. It is whether the idea is right enough for now. There is more than one way to do something, and if a method has the potential to get us there, why not try it? If that does not work, we can all regroup and reassess later.

I wrote a letter of support explaining that I believed it was an appropriate approach based on what everyone knew at the time. I also provided my team's proposal as a kind of alternative view, just in case it was needed.

But they were having a lot of trouble. Parts of the tunnel were still collapsing. Morale was low and there was a sense from the senior officials on site that rescuers were beginning to panic.

An hour or two later, on Day Four, Rahul called back and connected me with the secretary to the prime minister, who asked me to explain my thoughts. I did. He wanted me to be candid about how challenging the rescue mission was likely to be. I was.

At the end of the call, he asked me if I would come to the site to pitch in. And if I could come as fast as possible.

There was no job description and no contract, my help voluntary, but the mission was clear. Join the team and help in any way I could. I promised I would.

CHAPTER TWO

GET TO THE CHOPPER

Sitting in a hotel in Slovenia, observing the situation from afar, I was becoming more and more concerned with each passing hour. I abandoned the remainder of my trip and organised to travel to India.

I already had a multi-entry visa for India. As it turned out, I was meant to be going there later in the year to a meeting in Mumbai, so I could get into the country straight away.

Getting there was not an easy feat. Air travel in these post-Covid lockdown times is unpleasant enough when attempting a simple trip between, say, Melbourne and Sydney. If the flight departs even vaguely on time, it can be considered a win. Trying to get from Slovenia in central Europe to India, however, is not a simple one-stop journey with services every hour, on the hour. Far from it.

As I sat in the airport, waiting on a delayed plane, I stared out the window to the snow-capped mountains on the horizon. I realised that those awe-inspiring peaks I could see in the distance were essentially connected to India.

If you look at a map, the Swiss and Austrian Alps – with just a little bit of imagination – are linked to the Himalayas. I could have walked east along them to the tunnel site if I wanted to, if I was physically fit and crazy enough, and if time was not of the essence. No directions or GPS necessary.

In many ways, the whole world is connected geologically. And at that moment, I felt instantly connected to those forty-one young men trapped in a small cavern inside a mountain, while physically joined to the mountains I was peering at in the airport.

I'm going to get these men out, I thought to myself. I had an inexplicable and illogical but utterly overwhelming sense that we could achieve the impossible.

I flew from Ljubljana in Slovenia to Dubai in the United Arab Emirates, then from Dubai to Mumbai, from Mumbai to New Delhi, then finally from New Delhi to Dehradun.

On that final flight, I deliberately selected a seat on the left-hand side of the plane. This offered a perfect view of the Himalayas as we approached Dehradun. The landscape had transformed from almost entirely flat ground to soaring mountains.

The mountains grew bigger and taller as we flew. I watched in wonder as rivers flooded out of them, weaving narrow paths through creases and crevices at first then widening into vast bodies of water as they reached the floodplains of northern India. Once there, almost resembling braided hair from above, they spread out for hundreds of kilometres, bringing life and fertility to the middle parts of the country.

'Bloody hell,' I muttered under my breath. This part of the world really does put you in your place.

It was an exhausting journey, yet I did not feel fatigued. Not even a little bit. I felt completely calm and tuned in to the task that would await me in a few hours' time.

It was an almost eerie sensation that was difficult for me to comprehend, and one of several strange coincidences and out-of-character sensations that had begun months before the tunnel collapse and would persist through the following epic two weeks.

On approach to Dehradun Airport, like an ageing superhero, I snuck into the aircraft equivalent of a phone booth at 10,000 feet – the toilet. I shed my normal Arnold clothes and transformed with the help of my fetching costume – high-visibility pants, steel cap boots and a bright orange top.

While not quite the Superman suit, it meant I could step from the plane and be ready to engage with the mountain immediately.

A group of soldiers was waiting for me as I got off the plane. I was taken aback. I was not expecting an escort, much less from a team of specially trained elite soldiers.

'Professor Dix,' one said in a simple greeting, taking me by the arm.

A few of his colleagues grabbed my bags. Among them was a big case with all my rescue gear inside it. Why I had packed that to go on a trip that did not require it, something

I had no way of knowing I would desperately need, is one of those peculiar coincidences I mentioned earlier.

I was dragged to the front of long and winding queues of weary travellers. My bags were hurriedly shoved through an X-ray scanner meant to accept small hand luggage only.

'No time,' one of my military escorts explained. 'We will make it fit.'

They did, but I am not sure how they didn't jam the machine in the process. The security staffer watching the monitor furrowed his brow. Concerned, he gestured at a coloured shape, bright red, screaming out at him.

'Steel-capped boots,' I offered. He shook his head and ushered us on.

Two army guys practically carried me through the rest of the airport. We were as close to running as you can get, in a scene that would not have been out of place in an Olympic speed-walking competition.

Outside, it was a short walk to the air force base that occupied part of the airport. A helicopter was waiting, fully fuelled and warming up. I have been in plenty of helicopters before, having received my pilot's licence as a teenager and later trained to fly choppers. This one was not the latest model off the shelf.

It was huge but pretty old. I peered at the instruments panel and realised this thing was probably not much younger than I was. As we ventured closer to the tunnel site, the challenging terrain made itself known. It seemed we flew more up than along. The Himalayas rip straight up out of the Indian plains. Directly up. And so up we went, the ageing helicopter shaking violently as it struggled to reach the top.

God forbid something had gone wrong, because there were no flat spots on which to attempt an emergency crash landing. Just endless jagged rock and cliff faces.

As scary as it was, it was also kind of cool. I loved the Rambo films when they came out during the 1980s. I was also partial to Arnold Schwarzenegger action movies during that era.

Here I was, a very different kind of Arnie, being rushed to a chopper to tackle a high-stakes mission. That's where the similarities begin and end. I have not and never will have Schwarzenegger's physique.

We landed on a makeshift helipad, essentially some flattened dirt that the military had compacted down to allow helicopters carrying vital supplies and equipment to come in and take off from again. Rahul was waiting for me in a car.

'Do you want to go to the hotel to freshen up?' he asked, aware of the long journey I had just taken.

I shook my head. 'Take me to the tunnel.'

I could not tell you how long the drive was. My mind was preoccupied with thoughts of those forty-one men. We would get them out, I was confident. I have no idea why, though, given what I was about to see.

The site seemed chaotic. Rescue workers running to and from the mouth of the tunnel. Machinery screaming to life. Dozens and dozens of journalists, cameramen and photographers.

My first time in the tunnel was an overwhelming experience. The first thing I noticed were the scars of twenty-one prior catastrophic collapses inside. That was not good.

Had there been just one or two collapses, I could understand why work might have proceeded. But twenty-one? And in a long enough timeframe to fix the issues? It was totally incomprehensible to me why the tunnel had not been shut down until the situation settled and while the environment was carefully assessed.

This was a much bigger mess than I could have possibly imagined.

Not long after arriving at the site, I went to the top of the mountain to get a sense of what we were dealing with. There, it was peaceful and serene. The roar of machines, the frantic chatter of rescue workers, the clicking of cameras and the commentary of the press pack were a world away. I stood at the peak and looked out over the awe-inspiring vista beyond.

Beneath my feet was the worst kind of rock I could have hoped to find.

To understand a mountain like this, in this part of the world especially, you have to understand the environment's recent past. Recent in a geological sense, at least. So millions of years ago, not back in the nineties or something.

But not too long ago, the Himalayas were at the bottom of the ocean. When China and India crashed into each other, the mountains that now run between them were formed. In doing so, they ripped the seabed, thrusting it out of the water and into the air. That's why on the top of Mount Everest you'll find tiny sea shells.

Over time in this particular area, a series of folds, faults and compaction zones turned the ancient muddy seabed into rock. Well, barely rock. It is a very fragile and almost soapy rock. It is technically strong enough to build a tunnel through, if you do it carefully, but if that type of rock becomes unstable, it turns into a pile of soft rubble.

I ran my hands over the rock on top of the mountain. It disintegrated almost instantly. Just my gentle touch was enough to have solid rock fall into countless pieces. It is just that fickle. Terrible stuff.

I was surprised. I was not expecting the material to be quite so fragile. It was the last thing I hoped to find up there, because it meant many of the options we had come up with were going to be tough to implement successfully.

The signs of multiple severe collapses inside the tunnel, coupled with the overwhelming presence of this horrible rock, were very worrying. I went to a meeting with the senior officials leading the rescue, specialist engineers and geologists along with government officials and project executives, at the end of my first day on site.

Someone snapped a photograph of that first discussion – a shot that has now become quite iconic. There I am, at a table surrounded by people, with a piece of this crumbling, fragile rock in my hand. Even though my physical being is frozen in a split-second moment in that photograph, it is clear that I was quite animated.

The reality of it is that I was trying to explain, in a polite and diplomatic way, that the situation was fucked. Pardon my French. But it was truly fucked.

'We can't rush. The whole thing is going to collapse. There is no stability here on our rescue side,' I explained.

There was not just a risk of the trapped men being killed by what we were doing, but of all of us perishing, too.

'Look at this rock. It's barely rock. And twenty-one prior collapses? This is extremely dangerous, gentlemen.'

It could not have been worse. We were dealing with a mountain that, at any given moment, could completely fall apart.

The officials sitting around that table did not have any specific tasks for me. There was no preconceived idea about what I might be able to bring to the table. They simply asked me to assist them in getting these men out and home safely to their loved ones.

'What are our chances?' I was asked.

I just felt that we could do it. No, not just felt it – I felt deep in my bones that we *would* do it. We'd get these men out.

The moment I walked back outside, a horde of reporters from the assembled press pack leaped on me. I was a pink man with a foreign accent who had just swept in from abroad on a helicopter, so they assumed I must know something. They wanted answers, having not received many concrete ones so far. So I gave them one.

'Forty-one men alive, no-one else hurt, all home by Christmas.'

They seemed surprised by how definitive I was in my assessment. It was as clear as a bell and that sound was very sweet to their ears. But the journalists seemed sceptical. Did I truly believe we could save these men?

'Absolutely. I promise you now, we're going to rescue these men. The mission is clear. Forty-one men are coming home and no one else is going to be hurt in the rescue.'

Somewhere in the back of my head, almost entirely drowned out by an unusual, assured sense of confidence, but just audible enough, a tiny voice whispered: *What the fuck are you doing?*

CHAPTER THREE

RIGHT WHERE I'M MEANT TO BE

When I arrived at the tunnel site in India, it felt like I had been preparing for this rescue all my life. I know that sounds really weird and a little bit crazy. But in reality, I needed everything I have ever learned for that enormous task.

I needed every bit of the personal skills I picked up as a kid, working in my parents' hotels. Learning to keep calm, to open up with body language – skills I honed while navigating drunken guests as a child – would prove invaluable. Later, I'd used those same skills as a lawyer, calming angry judges, and even with customers when I dabbled as a trainee hairdresser. Yes, a hairdresser. I took up the course so I could learn about foils and colours to entertain my kids and their friends during school holidays. But perhaps most important was my ability to de-escalate and refocus when things got heated – something I mastered in the courtroom as a barrister.

I needed to problem-solve on my feet amid fast-changing circumstances, which is what I do day in, day out, as a scientist and engineer.

And strangely, almost unbelievably, I needed every single scrap of information, every important contact and every new way of thinking I had just gleaned over the previous twelve weeks. Back before I even knew I would need it, when I thought I was merely on a spur-of-the-moment trip.

What happened in the three months before the rescue?

You are never going to believe me, but it is absolutely true. Out of the blue, I had this sudden idea that I should travel the world and learn everything I could about the most extreme underground environments and techniques.

More than an idea, it was an irresistible urge. The moment it popped into my head, I grabbed the notion with both hands and sprinted.

Without really knowing why or for what purpose, I was undertaking a global tour of the most dangerous and perilous parts of mining and tunnelling. Hearing the freshest thinking on digging, drilling and preventing everything from going wrong. Experiencing the most unimaginable landscapes and the harshest conditions. And talking to the most revered specialists in their fields who were at the top of their respective games.

I was in the middle of that adventure when India phoned.

I had no reason for doing it. I just desperately wanted to do it. I felt compelled to go, and so I did.

Those closest to me, both in a professional and personal capacity, were all of the impression that I was off pursuing a fanciful idea. There was no potential business in it, it was a flight of fancy, and it would cost a small fortune. What was I thinking? My wife Divina probably thought I was having a nervous breakdown or midlife crisis.

Honestly, maybe a small part of me agrees, because I still do not really understand the motivation behind it. I cannot explain it. But I felt strongly that I should go off and learn about as much extreme tunnel stuff as possible. It was like taking an in-depth refresher course.

I travelled to South Africa to visit the world's deepest gold mine, the Mponeng Gold Mine in the country's Gauteng Province. Since digging began in 1986, countless workers have burrowed some 4000 metres down into the earth. Operators plan to push further down in search of more gold reserves.

Travelling from ground level to the deepest part of the mine takes over an hour – an hour just to get down there! That really puts into perspective the scale of this operation. I had the opportunity to venture down more than 4000 metres, alongside the experts who work in those depths every day.

I was amazed by the sight of twisted and bent rock, which is continually shifting and collapsing. Mostly in small ways, but sometimes to a significant extent, as it last did in early 2020. A magnitude 2 seismic event led to a series of faults and three people were killed.

I went to Finland and to the research facility dealing with the latest techniques for drilling into extreme rock. Some of the technology and knowledge from that research facility ended up at the rescue site.

I went to the Colorado School of Mines in the United States to study some of their techniques for extreme mining. These include NASA-funded work for desired future lunar missions to go to the Moon to mine things that are non-existent, rare or tough to extract here, but in abundance there. A big one is tritium, also known as helium-3, which could provide a clean and efficient form of energy.

Earth has a magnetic field that protects us from tritium. The Moon does not, and so it's regularly swamped with huge amounts of helium-3. If we can harvest it and bring it back to Earth, it could allow us to produce nuclear energy in fusion reactors. It's not really radioactive so, in theory, we could have nuclear energy without the dangerous waste product attached. If we can somehow figure out how to mine it and get it back to our planet, there is enough of the stuff on the Moon to power the entire planet with decarbonised fusion energy for about 10,000 years.

Imagine that. There is such huge potential on the Moon. So much so, the world's superpowers are engaged in a brand-new space race. This time, it has nothing to do with capitalism versus communism and an expensive pissing contest between two brawling countries. It is entirely about energy and resources.

The USA, China, India, Russia, Japan, the United Arab Emirates and the European Union are all driving something of a 'space rush' for this era's new gold. Except this stuff is worth much, much more.

A tonne of gold would be worth roughly 80 million bucks, depending on the trading value on the day. A tonne of tritium, or helium-3? One. Billion. Dollars. Suddenly, the idea of mining on the Moon and the enormous logistical and financial headaches involved do not seem so far-fetched.

I went to New Zealand to learn about the latest in tunnel support – and was there for Diwali! I was dancing with the crowds on the first day of Diwali in New Zealand, before news of the collapse got to me. If you search my LinkedIn or Facebook, I even posted about it.

I then went to Germany to inspect the latest tunnel-boring machines, one of which we used at the rescue site. Then I went on to Slovenia, where I was meant to speak at a tunnelling convention.

And then, it seemed, fate stepped in. That was where I received the first phone calls for advice. I made the decision to voluntarily go and help on one of these calls while I was in Slovenia. I arranged my flights immediately.

This strange field trip, which did not seem to make any sense when I embarked on it, turned out to be the most brilliant decision I have ever made.

It meant that, when I got to the site of this major unfolding disaster, a whole host of information was front of mind. It meant I had on speed dial some of the smartest people on the planet when it comes to this stuff. It meant I had access to vital ideas, techniques and equipment, with tools that I could obtain quickly.

For months before the collapse, without knowing it and for no logical purpose, I was preparing for the risky work that I was about to encounter. It was like I was cramming for a really tough test at university.

It felt like I was meant to be there. I was a perfect fit for the scenario. It was evident to me immediately. And weirdly, I had everything I would need.

And I really mean *everything*. Before I left home on my tunnelling pilgrimage, I did something else I never normally do. Ever. I packed my rescue gear.

This puzzled Divina. I only ever travel with some bare essentials chucked into a carry-on bag. Always. I like my time spent in airports to be minimal and as efficient as possible. None of this checking-in-suitcases nonsense. And definitely none of that lost-luggage business, which seems to be a common feature of air travel these days.

I especially hate the idea of lugging big, heavy and cumbersome bags everywhere – onto trains, up and down narrow staircases, through the dirt and mud . . . God knows where. So if it cannot fit in a small bag I never have to relinquish, I am not taking it with me. No ifs, no buts.

'Love, I think I might take a big bag,' I told Divina about twenty minutes before I was due to leave.

'What? Why?' she asked, shocked.

She knows me well enough to appreciate that this suggestion was wildly out of character. After all, she had endured plenty of holidays with me wearing the same three shirts and pants, over and over again.

But something about this felt different. I had no idea why then, and I am still just as puzzled now. But I had an urge to pack everything I possibly could. I grabbed my King Gee work shirt and my Aldi high-visibility pants. I packed all my safety equipment. I even made some food rations and put those in.

It was not some premeditated idea. I never planned to take any of that stuff with me. I just did it at the last minute.

In the time since the rescue, I have spoken about this bizarre sequence of events, the seemingly inexplicable coincidences, to a few Hindu people. For them, what's so unbelievable to me is totally understandable to them.

The way they have explained it is that Hindus believe people are chosen by the gods to perform certain deeds on Earth. They are destined to fulfil a particular purpose.

That is obviously a somewhat confronting idea for me, a scientist. It is simply not how I normally roll. But at the same time, I have no way of explaining the months leading up to the rescue. And I certainly struggle to put into words – and definitely cannot reconcile in my mind – what happened in India.

Or at least, how I felt about it. How I still feel about it all.

If all this stuff I am about to tell you was not meticulously documented, if the details, vision and photographs were not verifiable on various platforms, I might be inclined to disbelieve it myself.

I would probably book myself in for a series of medical scans, sure that I had suffered some catastrophic event and invented a whole bunch of vivid memories that never happened.

But there it is. On social media, in the press, via the recollections of countless people. Me doing all these very odd things that, in hindsight, make such perfect sense.

Me being exactly where I needed to be. Me fulfilling some kind of destiny.

Me, a very rational person who doesn't believe in the concept of fate, or at least didn't think he did . . . living out my fate.

CHAPTER FOUR

OF ALL THE DAYS TO DESTROY A TEMPLE

The first thing I did when I arrived at the tunnel site – before inspecting the tunnel, before making my way to the top of the mountain, and before speaking to a single official – was to head to the temple.

On the plane heading to the Himalayas, I connected to the in-flight wi-fi internet and started researching the circumstances of the accident. The approval for the tunnel. Who was involved in the construction. The original plans. Whether anything strange geologically had been reported in the days and weeks prior. That kind of thing.

I came across a local news story about the collapse. It happened to mention that the operators of the tunnel project had removed a small, makeshift temple from just outside the entrance. This harmless and very important religious monument was not in the way, it was not hurting anybody, and yet it was ripped out.

For some stupid reason, someone sitting in an office somewhere decided that this makeshift temple should be taken away – and it was done the day before the landslide. On the eve of the holy festival of Diwali.

The local priests believed the reason for the catastrophe was that the gods were angry about a shrine made in their honour being removed. That's why the collapse occurred. The gods were sending a clear message and were determined to punish the humans over a sign of arrogance and disrespect.

Fair enough. That would piss me off, too.

While I was still on the plane, I sent a message to ask Rahul what was happening with the temple. Surely, someone had realised the error and made arrangements with the local priests to rebuild it. I was relieved in a way to hear it had indeed been put back up.

'Can I go there first?' I asked. Rahul said I could.

So the first thing I did after getting off the helicopter, climbing into a car and driving to the tunnel site was to pay a visit to the rebuilt temple at the entrance of the tunnel.

I did not go to my hotel. I never even paused to go to the bathroom, nor was I interested in taking some time out to rest from the horrendously long journey. I wanted to go straight to the temple.

I approached with my head bowed and fell to my knees. I closed my eyes but I was not really sure what I wanted to do or say next.

Then it dawned on me. On the plane, I had read a bit about the Hindu goddess Kali. She is the goddess of time, doomsday, justice and death. After studying her and the important role she plays in the Hindu faith, I believed that who I really needed to have a conversation with was Kali.

So much so that while flying to India I wrote to chief engineer Gupta (and this is the exact quote from my WhatsApp text):

Me: 'Maa Kali? Can I pay my respects when I arrive? I did my research – Kali is a strong character – I do want to pay my respects given the spiritual significance of the area – is that possible? Is it possible I be taken to a place first – to pay my respects?'

Gupta: 'Good morning, No mobile signals at tunnel site. Will arrange for Darshan of Maa Kali.'

I asked Kali some simple questions, because I felt like she was still undecided about what she might like to do.

If she wanted to kill those men, she would have done so already. If she wanted to teach us a lesson for the ignorance we mere mortals had displayed, by first daring to tear through the mountain then toppling over this very temple, she could have given us quite a powerful education. She had not.

At the same time, she was not letting us rescue these men. By the time I got there, it had been several days since the collapse. Nothing that had been attempted to free those forty-one workers had succeeded. Hopes were low and spirits were fading. Kali simply had not allowed us to progress.

So maybe, just maybe, she was still making up her mind. I asked her, calmly and politely, if she might consider my point of view before she decided what to do.

I first asked her forgiveness. I then asked her to allow us to carefully and respectfully work to get these innocent men out. And finally, I asked that none of us be hurt in the process.

You can *take us*, I told her. *You can take all of us one day, but please, not today. Not right now. It is not our time just yet.*

My biggest regret is not knowing on that first day that I should have taken my shoes off before kneeling at the temple. I did not realise that in the rush of the moment. I really should have, though. It makes perfect sense.

When you go to someone else's house, you take your shoes off at the front door. It is a basic sign of respect, right? It is a recognition of the fact that you have been invited into someone else's space. I really should have known.

At the time, I do not think I fully understood why I was so eager to go to the temple. I had no premeditated thinking about why I should make a gesture like kneeling and praying. After all, it was an act that was pretty foreign to me.

But I just knew it was the right thing to do. Or more than that, I was absolutely sure that I had to.

In hindsight, I am so glad that I had that instinct. The locals believe the disrespect of removing the temple the day before the collapse had angered the gods. On top of that, we were in one of the most sacred places in the world for Hindu people, with the tunnel linking two of the four most revered Hindu sites. You put all that together and kneeling at that temple was probably the smartest decision I have ever made.

After all, my mum taught me as a kid to always be respectful of the house rules – no matter whose house you were in. Take your shoes off, be polite, offer to help with the washing up. It was the least I could do in this case.

I kneeled at that temple in a sign of respect, thanks and hope before I went inside the tunnel. Every single time. It was a small thing to do but it made a big difference in ways I could not imagine.

At the start of each morning, I would get a small bunch of flowers from a local family in a nearby village. I would take the modest arrangement and put it in the left breast pocket of my work shirt. They were a different colour each day, symbolising the promise and hope of a new dawn.

I would stop at the temple at the entrance to the tunnel before going inside. I would split half of the bunch of flowers for the temple and keep the remainder for myself. My thinking was that flowers are a symbol of life and of hope, so I would offer some to the gods at the temple and retain some for myself, for good luck.

Inside the tunnel, I would go right down to where the landslide had occurred. I would push my back up against the wall of rubble, stick my hands in the rocks and sit quietly to listen to the mountain.

I would walk away with a certain level of assuredness that, while the mountain was collapsing, it was not going to collapse on us right now. I cannot really explain it, but this daily ritual delivered some peace of mind that we were good to proceed. It was an act inspired by decades of learnings shared with me by old-timers, who worked underground and had enormous respect for the power and danger of those surroundings.

I am no stranger to temples. Something few people know is that, at the entrance to every tunnel around the world, you will find a shrine of some kind. It does not matter where you are, in Australia or Nepal, the USA or Brazil, there is a deep respect held among those who go underground for the fact that really, when you think about it, humans are not meant to be there.

I have never been to a tunnel without one. The religion of the country does not matter.

Catholics have a patron saint of miners and tunnellers, among other dangerously and potentially deadly professions: Saint Barbara. She often features in these shrines, but not always. One at a Brisbane tunnel project at the moment has distinct Indigenous characteristics to it.

These shrines are obviously a throwback to ancient times, but no-one is quite sure where the ritual comes from or how it started. But they are there in recognition of the dangers of working underground, even in this modern age.

Do not get me wrong. It is not like most tunnellers or miners make a big song and dance about it. But most will give these shrines a respectful and discreet nod when they pass by it at the beginning of their shift. It is a brief moment of solitude.

There is even a World Tunnel Day, which is marked on 4 December each year, the Feast Day of Saint Barbara. The whole industry celebrates the occasion. Jump on social media the next time 4 December rolls around and check out the pages of project operators, engineering companies and mining conglomerates. You will probably find some recognition of the extraordinary achievements of those who work underground.

So temples and tunnels go hand-in-hand. It is a sign of respect for the danger of the work being done, and for the great power the environment has over the mere mortals daring to enter it.

In this case, not only was the mountain shown a deep level of arrogant disrespect, in the form of multiple ignored warnings, but the desecration of a temple built in honour of the gods just outside the tunnel would have angered them.

Within a day or so of my arrival onsite, we had a major breakthrough. The bigger pipe, able to carry more food, water and medicine, as well as a communications link, broke through to the other side. It was a huge deal.

The fact that this modest pipe did not encounter any of the same kind of immovable debris of metal and concrete that the auger had was pretty remarkable. Those present were just as amazed and elated as I was.

In excitement, they told me that my act of kneeling at the temple before doing anything else must be responsible for the good fortune we had received. They believed that the change in fortune, after multiple failures and plenty of dashed hopes, was thanks to the respect shown to higher powers.

In doing what I considered to be the right thing – the bare minimum in a place where I was a guest and the temple was highly important – I had built a rapport with the rescuers.

I was not just some Anglo outsider infiltrating their operation. I was a man whose intentions were pure and entirely about saving those forty-one men.

CHAPTER FIVE

IN ANOTHER LIFE

Had I made one or two different decisions earlier in my life, if things had turned out just a little bit differently, I would never have taken that strange journey to unknowingly prepare for the greatest challenge I have ever faced.

I certainly would not have received a call from India's chief engineer. Hell, I would not even have half a clue who India's chief engineer was. And I definitely would not have jumped on a plane at a moment's notice.

In another life, in a parallel universe where an Arnold who is fairly similar to me exists, I would have probably been relaxing in a gaudy mansion in some posh Melbourne suburb, with an Italian sports car in a garish colour parked snugly in a four-car garage.

I almost certainly would have been wealthy. I am certain I would have been hugely successful as a barrister, and perhaps even working as a judge. But I am absolutely sure that I would have been miserable.

I was not exactly miserable when I started working with Gail Greenwood back in early 2000, but I was yearning for more from my life. I had reached a position many who had trod my professional path were desperate to claw their way to, and yet I was not overly fulfilled. I did good work in a great organisation, but it did not ignite any kind of fire within me.

I had no clue at the time, but finding Gail marked a major turning point in my life. And in her life, too, as it turned out.

Gail is one of those classic salt-of-the-earth people Australia is famous for. She is whip smart, straight down the line and doesn't take shit from anyone. Even me. She is compassionate but tough. She knows her worth but she is far from arrogant. She is fairly calm but God help anyone who wrongly assumes she is a pushover.

When she left school, Gail went to work for the State Savings Bank of Victoria. She worked there for seven years before getting married and buying a newsagency with her husband. They had a few kids and life was pretty good.

But both of her children were sick with chronic asthma. Her infant daughter's condition was so bad that the doctors feared she might not make it past three. While both kids were young and especially at risk of severe attacks, the family decided to move somewhere with a warmer climate than Melbourne's notoriously erratic weather provided.

They settled in Lake Boga on the Murray River in regional Victoria. It's only about three-and-a-half hours north of Melbourne by car, but it boasts 400 hours more sunshine than the actual Sunshine Coast does.

There, for five years, Gail ran a motel with a licenced restaurant attached. After that, she joined a local law firm in Swan Hill in a kind of office manager and secretarial role.

We met for the first time in 1993. Gail was overseeing some environmental cases and I was her firm's casual barrister. I would take on odd jobs for them, but did not need to visit the office too often. But a site visit was necessary that day, so I went to Swan Hill.

Gail recalls meeting me as being an unexpected and underwhelming experience. We had spoken on the phone plenty of times and she thought my voice was gorgeous. That's her word, not mine. We had a great rapport and got on like a house on fire for two people who had never laid eyes on each other.

I guess she had a picture in her head of what this intelligent and sophisticated young guy with a smooth voice might look like. It was not me. When she walked in and saw me sitting at her table, the illusion was shattered.

I had long curly hair and a big bushy beard. For some reason, I was wearing a safari suit a good two decades after it was vaguely fashionable to do so. She could not believe *this* was the bloke she had been talking to for so long.

But we worked really well together on that case, and again a few years down the track. That was it, though. Our paths did not cross again for many moons.

Eventually, with the kids older and less at risk, and with her husband scoring a job in Melbourne, they moved back to the big smoke. A recruiter phoned Gail not long after they arrived.

At the start of 2000, I was a junior partner at a massive law firm. I was burning through executive assistants at an alarming rate and the management was fed up. Now, let me be clear. I was not doing anything immoral, improper or illegal. I was just a pain in the arse to work for. I was quirky and unconventional, unlike anything a serious and revered firm was used to.

In eighteen months, four assistants had come and gone. In a bid to right the ship, and save money on mounting recruitment costs, the firm ordered that I take a psychological evaluation. They wanted to find the right personality who could work with me, and with whom I could work.

A small part of me also wonders if the firm was just really keen to make sure I was not absolutely, certifiably crazy.

At the same time, Gail was approached by a recruiter for a role as an executive assistant to a young and brilliant barrister doing some ground-breaking work in the environmental space. Again, those are not my words, but I'll gladly repeat them here.

But there was a catch. She had to do a psychological test to ensure we were compatible. Sceptical but intrigued, she agreed. We were a perfect match.

'Can I ask you a question?' she said to the recruiter. 'Is the guy I'd be working for Arnold Dix?'

Gail still laughs when she recalls how it sounded like the woman might faint. All her hopes of finally getting the right person for this nutter had seemingly vanished in an instant.

'So I guess you don't want the job anymore . . .' the recruiter sighed in defeat.

'No, no,' Gail quickly replied. 'That's fine. Just curious. We worked together a few times a decade ago and it sounded like it could be him.'

We were a dream pairing. Gail immediately got how I thought and how I worked. I would do what she described as my 'blue sky thing', running off at a million miles an hour, leaving debris and chaos in my wake. She would sort through the mess, figure out what needed to be done, and help me achieve it.

Some twenty-five years later, we are still together. It has been the most successful partnership. I cannot exist without her. She keeps the wheels on my fairly haphazard-at-times cart. And she is a big part of the reason why I have the exciting and full life that I do.

But back then, I was not sure what I wanted. Work was going well. I was switched on and could come up with an argument for just about anything. I was respected, both within the firm and in the broader legal community. And with Gail's exceptional administrative help, I had gone from the firm's worst-billing partner to its best in a year.

I had done some work with the New South Wales (NSW) Roads and Transport Authority. As a client, they were great to work with and seemed to enjoy the time they spent with me. They asked me to take on some more work, but the firm was solely focused on Victoria and did not want me spending too much time out of state.

I decided to move to another firm, Phillips Fox. Gail came with me, because we were now a package deal. You don't get me without her. She was keen to come and they were thrilled to have her talents.

One of their clients was the NSW Government, and one of the agencies I worked with was RailCorp. It was during an enormous period of planning and growth for Sydney's underground transport network, so I was excited to be across their files.

They called on 12 September 2001. Like the rest of the world, I was consumed by the shock and devastation of the images blaring nonstop from television screens and newspaper front pages. Two commercial aeroplanes had slammed into the towers of the World Trade Center in New York City, another into the Pentagon building in Washington, DC, and a fourth had crashed in a field in Pennsylvania.

My client wanted to travel to New York to inspect the subway tunnels that ran beneath the World Trade Center. They wanted to review what had happened that day, the series of events that occurred, at an operational level, when the planes hit those towers. They wanted to watch the recovery process that would shortly begin. They were desperate to glean every available lesson from this unprecedented but, as we now know, not impossible incident.

If the World Trade Center was to be the beginning of a wave of attacks, they wanted to be ready. Sydney was also to have a plethora of new road and rail tunnels running beneath it, so the authorities were determined to make them as safe as possible – whatever the circumstances.

I have seen plenty of death in my life. The nature of the kind of work I do is such that I cannot avoid it and, occasionally, I have had to witness it up close at its gory worst.

I have seen it so much in my life. I have been enveloped by the pain and misery it brings. That's part of my work. I have felt the pain of cities being attacked more often than most.

But the September 11 terrorist attacks completely destabilised me. I have never seen such senseless and unspeakable death. Investigating those tunnels beneath Manhattan that saved the lives of many people fleeing from the World Trade Center was soul-destroying.

It is hard for me to think too much about how horrible it was. I have never seen anything like that before, or since. I sometimes silently plead with the universe, in case it's listening, that I never have to again.

I was angry. I was deeply depressed. I had few words to describe the experience. It still hurts twenty-two years later, after I returned to Ground Zero for the first time since the disaster.

When I got home from that trip in 2001, I felt lost. I thought I had a clear picture of where I was going in life but, suddenly, I was rudderless. I had no clue what the path looked like.

I wrote the report for my client. It was largely positive, which almost made me physically ill. But the reality was that the evacuation procedures had worked well. Thousands of people were safely evacuated underground by train prior to the collapse. Only twelve people died in the underground on that horrid day; that figure could have been much, much higher if not for the systems and processes doing what they had been designed to do.

The twin towers underground evacuation job was done. It was time to move on. But I could not reconcile it within myself. There was no closure for me. I did not feel that I could move to the next faceless corporation that needed the services of a highly paid barrister within a mega law firm.

I wanted to do work that was focused on everybody, on the masses and the greater good, rather than a huge company and a few filthy rich individuals. I was instantly less tolerant of uncaring big business. I could no longer stomach the work.

I needed to find a purpose. I wanted to spend the rest of my life helping everyday, ordinary people – not one by one, but as the many.

Not long after that, I left the firm. I never went to work as a partner for another law practice again. I went out on my own to do work that might have a positive impact.

After leaving the security of a partnership at a law firm I voluntarily continued my focus on the safe operating design and procedures for major underground projects. This work has benefited hundreds, thousands, hundreds of thousands, or even billions of people. I have until this day continued with my voluntary international appointments on bodies that set the standards for underground safety. In 2022 I was recognised by the National Fire Protection Association (NFPA) of the United States with a special commendation – the Committee Service Award – which is the highest award for volunteers like me. It was a real honour as I am not American.

I have to admit, it is interesting, if not a little terrifying, to imagine where I might be had I not taken that course. In the space of a few short years, I completely upended my life and walked away from everything I had been working towards.

No more prestigious law firms. No longer on the fast-track to a high-profile career at the loftiest levels of Australia's legal profession. No more regular, fat pay cheque.

But what price do you put on living purposefully?

CHAPTER SIX

INNKEEPERS' KID WHO LOVED ROCKS

I was born in March 1964 to a pretty typical pair of rogues. My dad, Arnold John, immigrated from New Zealand and spent much of his early adulthood working as a used car salesman. He was a bit naughty. He had many of the characteristics that used car salesmen are famous for.

He was a smooth talker with the gift of the gab who could sell ice to an Inuit – for double the price they were used to paying.

My mum, Norma, was your quintessential country girl. She was down to earth, fiercely loyal and just a little hardened around the edges. After high school, she went off to study at the Emily McPherson College of Domestic Economy – a tertiary training institution for women that was founded in Melbourne at the start of the 1900s as the College of Domestic Science.

A generous grant from local businessman Sir William McPherson in the 1920s, roughly the equivalent of $2 million in today's money, took the modest but thriving school for young ladies and turned it into an educational force. It was renamed in honour of Sir William's wife, Lady Emily McPherson.

During World War II, it became a safe haven for women whose husbands had gone to fight abroad. It provided meals, shelter and skills training. In the shadow of peacetime, Mum enrolled and learned home economics and how to run a commercial kitchen.

The pairing of Mum and Dad made a delicious recipe for excitement. They fuelled each other's ambitions and wild streaks. Both came from very little but believed the world offered plenty of opportunities just waiting to be grasped.

And so, with a young family in tow, they set off to make money. They figured a sure-fire way of building business success was in booze, food and entertainment.

I grew up in hotels. Mum and Dad would snap one up, breathe new life into it, then sell and move on to the next project. From a young age, I was put to work in these lively establishments, clearing tables, collecting glasses, emptying ashtrays and washing dishes.

It provided a colourful and eye-opening education. I learned how to converse with grown-ups from all walks of life, and in varying states of inebriation. I cottoned on pretty quickly that if I was friendly and just a tad precocious, one of the old punters propping up the bar might flick me a coin as a kind of tip for a job well done.

My formative memories are of weaving through tables, chairs and barstools, feeding off the unique energy that courses through a suburban or country watering hole. Those years built the foundation of a work ethic that is so rock solid it borders on obsessive.

I suspect those experiences are to blame for my inability to sit still for too long. We were always on the move, with Mum and Dad in search of the next project and a fresh challenge. As a result, I went to six different primary schools across Victoria, New South Wales and the ACT – both regional and suburban. Primary schools in places such as Mount View, Cohuna, Benalla and Canberra can all claim me as alumni.

At some point, we ended up in Jindabyne, which at that stage was still a fledgling settlement sitting on the edge of the Snowy Mountains. There were no alpine fashion stores, no sprawling ski resorts nearby and not a great deal to do.

I would wander around aimlessly after school, looking for something – anything – to keep myself occupied and amused. It was during these years that I first crashed into tunnels and rocks.

All around Jindabyne, but usually in the front bar of Mum and Dad's hotel, you would find these old-timers with thick European accents, waxing lyrical about the old days. They had immigrated to Australia and the mountainous wilds of southwestern NSW to work on the Snowy Mountains Hydro-electric Scheme.

When the work was complete, they hung around. There was not much point in returning to Europe or venturing to some other part of Australia. They were content to hang around Jindabyne and wait for mortality to tap them on the shoulder.

Bored and probably intrigued by this kid confidently wandering around a pub all night, these blokes would strike up conversations with me. I would lean against the bar and listen to their stories about being part of this enormous nation-building infrastructure project.

I feel like every Australian broadly knows what the Snowy Hydro is, such is its significance. It imprinted itself on our national DNA, thanks to its scale, the huge benefits that flowed, and the sheer audacity of the plucky Aussies who proposed and championed it.

Like the Snowy Hydro, most of us have at least a vague understanding of the grand Murray River, which has been a life source for the towns and farming communities that sprung up in the 1800s. Development and diversion of the river over the past few hundred years has provided a vital source of water for humans, crops and animals.

In stark contrast, nothing had ever been done with the Snowy River; it was a real missed opportunity. This stunning body of water rises in the Australian Alps and flows through vast stretches of mountain country, before weaving its way through the Gippsland region in Victoria and out into the southern Pacific Ocean and Tasman Sea.

In the wake of World War II, in search of big-ticket infrastructure projects that could provide employment and economic stimulus, the NSW government came up with the idea of diverting the Snowy into the Murray and Murrumbidgee rivers. The sole purpose was to support agriculture and assist in the development and expansion of new communities.

South of the border, the Victorians had a better idea. The government chimed in with a proposal to use the Snowy, which boasts the highest headwater source of anywhere in the country, to generate electricity.

The federal government organised a committee to thrash out both proposals and produced a report in 1948 that laid the groundwork for the Snowy Hydro project. It would be another decade before consensus was found and an agreement reached. Waters flowing from the Snowy Mountains would be diverted to generate hydroelectricity, on top of providing irrigation to arid regions in the west.

For those who were not around at the time, you need to understand how big a deal this was. Australians were beside themselves with excitement about the Snowy Hydro. It was a huge project, almost absurdly ambitious in its big thinking, so that the reception to it was on par with an Olympic Games held Down Under or a visit from some of the more popular British royals.

The support for the project bordered on pandemonium, which is really what the country needed in the economic struggle of the postwar era.

Like all good Australian icons, from pavlova to Russell Crowe, Kiwis played a major role in the Snowy Hydro's formation – a contribution that has since been overshadowed. The chief engineer on the scheme was New Zealander William Hudson. His strong influence saw a massive number of workers recruited, predominantly from Europe.

Bringing together young migrants from dozens of countries, many of whom had not long earlier loathed each other after many long years of military conflict, is credited with sewing the multicultural fabric of Australia.

From start to finish, it took about twenty-five years to build the Snowy Hydro. It officially opened in 1974. It remains the largest engineering endeavour ever undertaken in Australia.

And it really is a beast. Across the whole complex, you will find nine power stations, sixteen dams, two pumping stations, a complex network of pipelines and aqueducts, and some 225 kilometres of tunnels.

This was my playground. Some kids love swinging from monkey bars and getting filthy making mud pies. For me, I was happiest when carefully stepping through a field or trawling along a riverbed, keeping my eyes peeled for any interesting-looking rocks.

Those old codgers who had worked on the Snowy Hydro took me on some incredible adventures, too. They showed me their old tools – worn shovels and blunted picks, rudimentary headlamps, and a collection of hand drills and wrenches. They snuck me into some of the tunnels, which was incredibly cool but fairly dangerous. When the water level at Lake Jindabyne dropped low enough, they would collect me from the pub and take me by boat to see the high points of the old town, which had been abandoned and flooded during the early construction phase.

Best of all, they would explain in detail the most interesting items in their rock collections. These guys were just as obsessed with geology as I was. They had given themselves an education on all things rocks while digging and tunnelling, despite many having missed out on formal schooling during the war in Europe.

And then there was something even more profound. These were World War II refugees – men and women who had once been enemies of each other, and of Australia too. Some spoke of actually seeing Hitler; others told stories of getting swept up in the frenzy of Third Reich rallies. They even joked about having shot at each other, all of it shared over laughter and much beer. Now, they were friends, celebrating together in their new home – Australia.

It was in that pub, among these once-bitter foes, that I learned about diversity, equity, inclusion, and tunnels – cheers to that!

Earlier in my childhood, at the Victoria Hotel in Benella that my parents ran in regional Victoria, one of the old-timers who lived upstairs passed away peacefully in his sleep. He had no next of kin, no family members who could come to collect his possessions, so Mum and Dad went through the room carefully and respectfully.

Any clothing in good nick was donated to the Society of Saint Vincent de Paul. A small amount of money was given to the local church. And a box in the bottom of the rickety old wardrobe in the corner of his room went to me.

I opened the lid. It was full of rocks this bloke had diligently collected over the years. I marvelled at the assortment. It was like finding a pirate's treasure chest.

I got to work on trying to identify as many of them as I could. It ignited a fire inside of me. I became obsessed with what lay beneath my feet in the depths of the earth. I completely fell in love with rocks.

I have a vivid memory of being about nine or ten, driving in the car somewhere with Mum. As we whizzed down the highway, a faint glint in the distance caught my eye.

'Stop!' I screamed. She jolted in panic, almost veering off the road. 'Let me out!'

She obliged, albeit with no idea why. I leaped out the door and sprinted across a patch of dirt to where I thought I had spotted that brief flash of a reflection from the sun. After a few moments leaning over, scanning the ground carefully, I found it. It was a chunk of olivine, a rare mantle rock found in only a few places on Earth – one being the western districts of Victoria.

I skipped back to the car triumphantly. With a grin from ear to ear, I held up my prize to show my still-confused mother.

'Wooooooow,' she said, trying her best to sound excited. 'Can we get back on the road now?'

After high school, I studied science at Monash University in Melbourne. I felt so lucky to be able to sink my teeth into this area that I absolutely loved.

The course I got into was pretty competitive. It is remarkable to consider that, not too long before, I was a remedial student at risk of slipping through the cracks, and now I was entering a course with a higher entrance requirement than engineering. Back then education was also free, so a lot has changed.

At uni, I was Mister Straight. While it was a particularly loose time to be a student on an Australian university campus, with a lot of drug-taking, sex and troublemaking, I abstained from the drugs.

I did not judge the drug-takers though. I did not struggle with being around all that action. In fact, it was pretty funny to watch. Especially the regular 'mega bong' competition that was a rite of passage for most students.

If you are not of my vintage, you did not go to a uni at that time, or your uni was a bit less irresponsible than mine, let me enlighten you. The mega bong competition was a true test of wit and strength. Basically, the challenge was to be the final person who was conscious after everyone sucked on a bong for as long as they could, until they were out of breath and fainted.

One by one, each stoner would collapse until there was just a solo competitor left standing. Well, kind of standing. Awake at least. So dumb. So incredibly funny to watch.

It just was not for me. I have never smoked marijuana. I have never taken drugs. I am a teetotaller.

I went back to Monash recently. It is a hugely impressive place, but a small part of me was depressed by how sensible modern students are. There is no sign of anyone behaving badly like they did back in my day.

They probably get a lot more done than my era of students did, though.

I fancied myself as a bit of a mad scientist, too. This did not always put me in good standing with the university. Take the day I caused the evacuation of the first-year chemistry labs. Although, really, the true blame lay with my old friend, the exothermic reaction.

First-year chemistry was pretty boring and straightforward. They wanted us to do some kind of tame experiment, but I had a better idea. I could try something a bit more challenging, involving an exothermic process, which in simple terms is something that releases energy in the form of heat, smoke and, with some luck, fire.

Unfortunately, it got a little out of hand. The reaction produced a heap of different gases. The fume cupboard, which should have contained any chemical mishaps, could not cope. Everyone had to flee.

My group got marks taken off as a result, which made me pretty unpopular among that particular cohort of peers.

It was clear that a future in chemistry was never going to happen. My attitude was not what was needed for a job like that – I was a bit too cavalier. Luckily, I was really into earth sciences, so I leaned into geology. I tapped into that boyhood love of rocks and the planet, and the fact that this huge mass we sit on, hurtling through space, is very much alive.

During my postgraduate studies, I went to Ranger Uranium Mine in the Northern Territory. It was a remarkable time to be in that part of Australia. I had never really seen anything quite like it.

While I was out surveying the landscape one day, I came upon an old cave. This beautiful and peaceful space overlooked the floodplains below. Just inside the entrance was a rock that looked like it had been carved into a chair.

Seriously, it was like an armchair. You could pick it up, plonk it in your house and, aside from being made of rock, it would make a great piece of furniture. It was the perfect place to sit and ponder the world in one of the most beautiful places I have ever been.

When a massive storm rolled in across Magella Creek floodplains, that is exactly what I did. I sat there in an armchair made of rock that, presumably, Indigenous people had perched in for tens of thousands of years before.

It was a perfect experience. Sitting there, I watched the dark clouds bring drenching rain to the landscape below. I watched blinding lightning and listened to ear-piercing thunder, the crackling echoes of which ricocheted off the cave walls.

This is incredible, I thought to myself.

I felt an overwhelming sense of place. I felt a deep connection to the land, to the natural world. It was a powerful moment that has stuck with me ever since. Seeing the enormity of nature, its beauty and might, realising that it has the ultimate say on how we live – and for how long we survive – left its mark on me.

I spent months in Kakadu conducting research, but this is where my whole career started to become wobbly.

The work I was doing indicated that the protection of Kakadu National Park, which had only just been given World Heritage status, required an understanding of the naturally occurring distribution of heavy metals and radionuclides. I will not bore you with the intricate details of my findings, but essentially, my research suggested that the natural variability was far greater than what anyone had previously acknowledged.

It meant that the claims by federal regulators and the Office of the Supervising Scientist that everything was fine, that mining uranium would be straightforward, risk-free and not have any kind of ramifications, was wrong. It was somewhat optimistic because they really had no idea what the baseline situation was.

But at the same time, the claims environmental groups had made – that everything was horrible and this entire project should not proceed – were also not based on fact.

The reality of the situation was far more complicated than anyone realised or cared to admit. I shared my findings, expecting that maybe I would be seen as clever and helpful. Instead, everyone had their metaphorical guns pointed at me. No-one was happy.

Of course, the authorities ignored my findings. So I went public with them and made a submission to a senate inquiry into the uranium mining operations. Not long after that, I had a visit from some shady people from the government.

I have no idea what department or agency they represented, but they were your stereotypical men in dark suits with dark sunglasses. They took me to one side and suggested that I shut up or I would probably never get a job as a scientist in Australia.

At that stage, I was a junior. I lacked the power and name to be able to hold my own. And I was working in a government facility. The threat was real.

Rather than shut up, however, I decided to study law. If that is how people react when I tell the truth, I figured, I would just do something else. And I would do something where I could be a troublemaker, shouting about something important and shining a light on those who would prefer darkness to prevail.

I really enjoyed studying law. This sounds hugely arrogant, but I found it kind of easy. I could not get my head around why other students complained about how complex things were. To me, it seemed like a huge and hilarious secret that law was, in fact, quite straightforward. I was sure a bunch of lawyers must have got together at some point in the past and made a pact to convince the world that law was this impossibly difficult thing.

In reality, there is not even any fundamental truth to it. It is not like when you build a rocket and it either goes up or blows up. It is not like building a house that either stands the test of time or collapses in on itself. The law is one big thought experiment and you can kind of push it wherever you need it to go.

I did quite well at that. I figured that I would devote my life to the law, but that I could weave some scientific and environmental elements into my practice.

Dad taught me how not to behave as a father and husband. I think he was a really insecure man. He always wore a lot of gold and had to have the best of everything. In particular, the fastest and most expensive car. And I'm pretty sure I have more brothers and sisters than I have met.

He was all the things that I am not. I take much more after my mum. Mum is fiercely into justice and what is fair. She gives everyone a fair go and never judges, instead seeing the best in everyone.

Actually that's not entirely true. Once she takes a position on an issue she is also judge and executioner – fair, yes, but if she decides your best is not good enough, beware. But she is all about the truth. Do not lie to Mum. She will find out and she will be pissed off.

As a publican, Mum was brilliant at holding a crowd. She could get along with anyone, she was great at cracking jokes, she was very down to earth and unpretentious. And hell, could she tell a story. I have never met a yarn-spinner quite as talented as her.

One of the best things she instilled in me was the value of having a go. She supported me no matter what, regardless of what I wanted to pursue. I knew that from a young age. Her only condition was that I never half-arsed whatever I was doing. I had to give it everything I had.

By comparison, Dad was pretty disappointed when I came home and announced I was heading off to university. As far as he was concerned, I was an innkeeper born and bred. As a kid, I was really good at cleaning ashtrays, clearing dishes, pulling beers, connecting the kegs in the cellar, doing food preparation in the kitchen – all of that.

Suddenly, I was turning my back on this profession he had been preparing me for. He was not pleased. I think he wondered what he had done wrong in raising me.

I am grateful for those experiences. That is absolutely where I get my work ethic from. My family was the epitome of working class – working hard, sacrificing so much, never complaining. They just got shit done. Now I get shit done, too.

And I think Dad might agree that it is a bit more exciting and rewarding than cleaning ashtrays. Maybe.

CHAPTER SEVEN

LISTENING TO THE MOUNTAIN

Those old miners in Jindabyne who were responsible for sparking my love affair with tunnels and most of the veterans I worked with as a training geologist all shared a remarkable respect for the landscape.

They were humbled by nature and its enormity, and they accepted the reality that, despite the great lengths they went to control it, it was ultimately nature that rolled the dice.

In some form or another, they had each seen what nature is capable of. Glory, yes, beauty, absolutely, and life-sustaining generosity, without question. But they also faced the ever-present risk of mere mortals being overpowered and beaten by the natural world.

Flooding rains, destructive cyclones, crushing earthquakes, relentless bushfires, unstable mountains, unpredictable landslides . . . you name it, Mother Nature has got it. Those who guided me into the world of geology had seen the very best and absolute worst, particularly when working underground.

As a kid in Jindabyne, I observed a practice that I would adopt and carry on for decades to come. One of the old Snowy Hydro workers was leading me on an adventure along a scarred, jagged cliff face to the entrance of one of many tunnels that had been dug for the project.

Before we entered, he became very quiet, as though standing in awe in a marvellous cathedral. He crouched down, his back and knees creaking as he did, and sat with his back against the rock. There, with his eyes closed, he carefully slid his hands into the soft ground, covering them up to the wrist with dirt, sand and bits of rock.

'Listen to the mountain,' he instructed. 'You should always listen to the mountain. She will tell you a lot if you're willing to pay attention.'

After several moments of quiet reflection, the man opened his eyes and a gentle smile spread across his heavily lined face.

'We may go in now.'

Some of the older geologists I encountered early in my studies and career had similar, almost-identical rituals. They too would feel the earth around them to see if there was something it wanted to say.

Long before technology existed to give precise and detailed readings of the murmurs and minute movements of a mountain or underground space, bare hands, listening, smell and an open mind were all these men had.

And they figured out how to listen respectfully to what was being said. They taught me how to use my hands and my body to 'listen' to the mountain. My senses are not the only tool I rely on when working underground, of course. But I have not discarded them simply because this is not taught in this modern age.

Before the collapse inside the Silkyara Bend–Barkot tunnel on 12 November, twenty-one prior collapses had occurred in that same section of tunnel. Twenty-one. Even people unfamiliar with working underground, with no experience of tunnelling into a mountain, would surely recognise how big that number is.

Those collapses were evident the moment I first entered the tunnel. Its interior was covered in deep scars from recent injuries, stretching right from the entry to the point of the collapse.

I could not fathom how there could be so many serious and alarming incidents without work being halted. One collapse? Maybe you would assess and make a call to continue. Two collapses? I would feel cautious about doing anything else without being absolutely sure that the structure was safe.

But three, four, five, six, seven, eight, nine . . . and so on? It seemed absurd to me that the whole project had not been shut down.

I do not want to criticise anyone or call into question what should and should not have been done. Others have done that. There have been investigations and reports. But it really goes without saying – and it beggars belief – that ignoring the clear warnings the mountain was giving was a mistake.

The mountain had expressed its dissatisfaction. What was happening inside it was not right. It was making it clear, repeatedly and with growing anger, that something would have to give sooner rather than later. And then it did.

The change that takes place across the Himalayan landscape from autumn to winter does not happen in one fell swoop. Rather, the scenery shifts gradually, with a transformation washing over the forest gently like a piece of satin running through fingers.

The vibrancy of evergreen leaves becomes a little duller, and the vivid oranges and yellows of deciduous trees start to fade in preparation of the colder months.

Even the light casts itself differently on the peaks. When the days become shorter, there's something almost romantic about how the afternoon sun casts itself on the crinkled expanse of rock below. It's careful – not harsh like it might be in the depths of summer.

A lot of the plants in this part of the world have autumn flowers blooming on them. Most days, I would go out to collect a small handful, either to put in my pocket and take to the temple, or just to hold for a brief moment. A reminder of the beauty that still exists in the world, even when it seems as though things feel desperately bleak at times.

These small flowers were pretty and delicate. They were not ostentatious or abrupt in their beauty, but understated. Even the sweet aroma they gave off was not the potent or overwhelming kind. It was just enough.

The forest in India is nothing like the bush in Australia. At home, the wild is really heavy. That is the best word I can think of to describe it. Those who bushwalk will know what I mean – off the beaten track is a dangerous place to be. But here? You can wander through the natural landscape, among and beneath the trees, and not feel as though you might be swallowed.

It almost feels like you have shrunken down in size to live inside a carefully constructed terrarium.

Most days, just before dusk and in the hour before dawn, the wind would pick up a little and whoosh its way through the valleys. The sound the trees made as their branches and leaves danced in the breeze is unlike anything I have ever heard before.

It sounded like the mountains were breathing. I would often find a quiet place to sit for a few minutes, alone and away from the hustle and bustle of the rescue site, to listen to this gorgeous sound as night became day.

I cannot quite explain it, but the mountains felt welcoming. Almost instantly. It was unusually familiar, too, as though they were giving me a warm embrace – like an old friend greeting you after a long time between visits.

I felt pretty undeserving of the affection.

From the moment I set foot on the ground, I felt conflicted about my role here. I was trying to reverse the consequences of something that, in a strange way, felt almost understandable. The collapse of the tunnel, I mean.

Of course, no-one would wish that kind of horror on their worst enemy, let alone forty-one innocent men. But the mountain was doing its thing, the thing it had always done before people came along, and we – us humans – had disturbed it.

On the one hand, the ambition to build connections for pilgrims between sacred temple sites was extremely noble and worthy. But on the other, we were scarring this incredibly beautiful stretch of nature with our modern wants – to make ourselves happy, to live fuller lives.

I felt really torn. I understood the benefits of putting a tunnel through this place, but I was moved by just how awesome it was. It felt intrusive for humans to be here, acting in such a disruptive and permanently altering way.

Really? We have to do it here? Right here?

My emotional response to the place was pretty complex. I am an engineer and a scientist. I am used to being tuned in to technical, rational scenarios. Here is a problem; here is how we will fix it using our smarts and ingenuity. Now, there were heavy layers of importance linked to the sheer bloody beauty of the environmental surroundings. And they felt just as important to acknowledge.

If you ever have the opportunity to do so, I encourage you to take a walk through the Himalayas at night. If you ever have the prospect of doing so, you must. As remarkable as this part of the world is during daylight hours, you should see it in the dark. Absolutely spectacular.

Sometimes, I would sneak off from the main camp and carefully make my way up to the top of the mountain – much to the horror of those who were meant to be guarding me. After finding a spot to sit, I would slump down and stare upwards through the gaps in the trees at the exploding universe above. When not suffocated by city lights, the sky is almost blinding. A million specks of light and swirls of vibrant colour against an inky black backdrop.

I cannot guess how many hours collectively I spent up there on my own in the darkness. Well, not completely alone. I had my geophone to keep me company. A geophone is a precise device that listens to rock. Think of it as a heart rate monitor that keeps track of the life of a mountain.

Amid the peace, all kinds of animals find the courage to creep out from wherever they shelter to explore their evening surroundings. Monkeys. Deer. I swear I saw a puma one night out of the corner of my eye in the shadows.

During those quiet moments, those rare breaks away from the chaos down below, I could stop, catch my breath and reflect. It was an honour, an enormous privilege, to be here. I felt special. It was not that I felt entitled, but I did have a sense that I was invited. I was here with a purpose, rather than simply as a tourist.

I was an honoured guest, of sorts. And I felt very humbled to be so.

I have never experienced such a collective resolve of multiple agencies, of experts from all manner of fields, to work together towards a common mission as during the rescue.

Whenever we would get together, it was kind of chaotic. At first, I was taken aback by how meetings are run in India.

On the face of it, you could take it as everyone just yelling at each other.

But it is deliberate. That is how things get done.

From the moment we sat down around the table, everyone's opinion was being sought, listened to and tested, concurrently. All at once. Somehow, it worked. After thirty or forty minutes of excited chatter, we would reach some kind of landing point – a few options that we agreed on.

Indians believe in listening to every voice – usually at the same time.

I have never witnessed this emotional enthusiasm in another professional setting. It is incredible. You are absolutely immersed in the discussion, swimming in all kinds of different ideas.

It can feel unruly if you are not used to it. It can seem as though everyone is talking over the top of everyone else. But in reality, it is like a perfect harmony – different notes coming together to compose a melody that somehow works.

Everyone is heard. Each suggestion is considered. In the end, there is a consensus.

We were a motley crew. Engineers, scientists, politicians, local experts, bureaucrats from far away and some pink guy with a bushy beard. And yet, these meetings were successful. Each day, as a group of professional men and women, we would reflect, learn and move forward.

Those meetings really taught me that intelligent and informed decision-making doesn't have to look like it does in Hollywood films. It doesn't need to resemble a shiny

With my dad Arnold John Dix at the house Mum and Dad built in Lusk Drive, Vermont, Melbourne, in March 1964.

With my Auntie Gloria out the back of my mum's family cafe in Cohuna, Victoria, in 1964.

With my nana Elsie on her first overseas trip in 1965 to visit my dad's parents in New Zealand. She had never travelled before – we jointly smuggled silver coins back to Australia in my soiled nappy.

From left, myself, bear (an alcohol brand promotion) and brother Colin in front of our first microwave oven in the Jindabyne Hotel in 1973. Working in the kitchen and clearing was normal for kids.

A young me in 1974 heading off to a family wedding.

On a geology field trip in 1983 in Mansfield, Victoria. I found a huge fossil lungfish – bliss.

At my graduation from law at Monash University in 1988. What a sexy bloke!

My Law Society class photo in 1988. I liked to be formal at Law school. My tie came from my cousin Sandra and the suit from the Boronia op shop in Melbourne.

A family drive in the Dandenong Ranges in my prized Land Rover Series I, with (from left) me, Sam, Karen and newborn baby Hannah.

Inspecting the tunnels that were successfully used to evacuate people from the Twin Towers before they collapsed after the September 11, 2001 terrorist attack.

Inspecting rolling stock at New Jersey Transit in September 2001. People were brought under the Hudson River during the Twin Towers evacuation.

Reading about the suspected anthrax attack while I was in New York on 17 September 2001. My world changed.

My kids (from left) Edward, Hannah and Sam in Sydney in 2002, with a RailCorp underground fire rescue truck. I always tried to include my kids in my work.

My kids training to use fire hoses – for real.

Gail and I in Brussels in 2007 when we were special experts to the European Parliamentary Enquiry into the assessment of the safety of tunnels.

Diving in the Solomon Islands, collecting evidence for a court case on mining pollution in 2008.

In 2008 Gail and I were in Albania, where I survived a couple of politically motivated assassination attempts. Here you can see old upturned military pillboxes with (from left to right) Gail, our interpreter, and the head of police who captured my would-be assassins.

With Taiwan's Prime Minister Ma Ying-jeou discussing Taiwan's typhoon disaster response in Taiwan in 2012.

A tunnel safety briefing for safety officers at Hamad International Airport, Qatar, in 2014.

In 2015 in my role as the *Guinness World Records* tunnel verifier in Qatar for their world record attempt for having the most tunnel-boring machines running at the same time.

My daughter Hannah and my now-wife Divina working together in a tunnel in Qatar in 2017.

In 2017 the Grenfell Tower fire had me working in London to help investigate the scandal of it happening, given a similar fire had occurred in 2009 in Lakanal House, South London. I appeared in the coronial inquiry into the Lakanal House fire.

boardroom full of suited and rigid men. It can be a bit Bollywood-style.

If our hearts were clear and our minds were focused, we believed we could succeed. We had a pure mission. No-one had a goal to be right, to have the loudest voice, to take credit for success or deflect blame for failure.

It was simply about getting forty-one kids home by Christmas, without anyone else being hurt in the process.

Being up in the Himalayas was remarkable. It does feel like a different planet – an alien landscape dreamed of by many but traversed by a lucky few. If ever there was a place where something seemingly impossible was going to happen, it would be here. It looms large. It wraps you up and consumes you, making you part of the space.

The sounds of the trees, the wind weaving through those mountains and the way the landscape almost seems to breathe, is magical. You understand why gurus hang around up there.

It is the youngest set of mountains on Earth. Even though they look really old, this is one of the places where the lift of the planet is most active. They are brand-new. They are still popping up right now, which is what makes them so unstable.

Mountains in Australia are like old farts. Mount Kosciuszko is a snoozefest. She has had her time and now she is sleeping. Forever. She is ancient. If you have ever been there, I am sure you have felt it.

But up in the Himalayas? It is positively alive. It puts you in your place. You are delivered a heavy dose of humility.

They are not just some big piles of rocks. They are active and constantly moving. Alive.

When I would go to where the collapse was occurring, I would always go right up to the wall of fallen rocks, push my back up against it, against the remnants of the tunnel wall, and bury my hands into the earth. I would take a few minutes to sit and listen to the mountain.

Can I hear it cracking? Can I feel it rumbling? Are there fresh movements to be felt? How does it smell? Is there more water now than before? What is the mountain trying to tell me about what is happening here?

While I listened carefully to the mountain, however, I have to admit that I failed to listen to one or two directives from rescue authorities.

When I first got to the tunnel, the only directive the bigwigs gave me was that I could not stay onsite in the army camp. I think they felt it would be inappropriate, given I was a volunteer and guest of the government.

I guess they felt I should behave more like a bureaucrat. A white shirt versus an orange one, if you like. Or a green camouflage one, in this case.

But I was reassured that, in Indian culture, it is OK to not do as you are told provided you do not wind up humiliating the person you are disobeying. What is important is that you *were* told. The person giving the directive assumes you are an adult and will make the right choice.

So each night, I ignored the one big rule I had been given. I would go back to the hotel with everyone for dinner. We would debrief over a shared meal, consisting of several pots of aromatic food placed on the buffet table against the wall, forensically analysing the day that was and briefly discussing what tomorrow might bring.

It was more of a boarding house than a hotel. Everyone was lovely and happy to see us, but it was pretty basic in a Western sense. The hotel staff were especially kind to me – often cooking the vegies I liked and even switching on my room's little hot-water system before I got back from camp. It was a sacred place with only vegetarian food on the menu in this region.

I would go upstairs with everyone else, have a quick wash, change back into the same clothes, then sneak back to the site. The army had tents set up and I was given a camp stretcher in one with a bunch of officers.

Like most other parts of the world, the real work is done when management is not looking. If I really wanted to find out what was going on, I knew I had to be onsite at night-time when the other white hats were not.

That meant working through the night then sleeping with the army guys when I could. It was a bit like a Scouts camp. They were really nice and extremely professional. They welcomed me with open arms. Everyone involved with the rescue was fantastic. That was an unusual experience for me.

I have been in plenty of rooms where there is at least one dickhead. You know the type. For whatever reason, whether they are scared or feel stressed, they are arrogant or dismissive or controlling. And the more they feel that way, the louder they become at that table.

But this was incredible. Somehow, probably just through great luck, we did not have a single dickhead. Everyone got along. Everyone was on the same page about what was at stake and how important it was for us to work together. And we all had each other's backs, too.

Because of how the law is practised these days, because of how adversarial it tends to be, lawyers and their tactics have almost paralysed smart people from doing smart things. They wind up being worried that, if something goes wrong, they will be punished for it.

The same can be said for India. No-one expressly voiced their concerns about liability, legal consequences or anything like that. But I was sure it had to be weighing on some minds. So in the meeting room, I tried to strike a tone that eased some of those fears.

'Do we all agree that we don't have enough information at this stage to make a decision?' *Yes*.

'Do we all agree that if we do nothing, those men will eventually die?' *Yes*.

'So let's do something we think might help, even though there's a chance it won't.'

I pledged to the men and women in my team that, no matter what, I would have their backs. If anything went wrong, I would always make clear that the decision we made was correct based on all the information we had.

Basically, if you go down, I go down with you.

That declaration, my willingness to step up and stand shoulder-to-shoulder with them all, infected the room. It created a team mentality and united those around the table. It allowed us to examine proposals clearly and assess them purely on the likelihood of success – not of a lawsuit. As a lawyer I was enabling my co-professionals to do their jobs unshackled from the fear of being sued. I was doing what all good lawyers should do – helping other professionals be and be seen as professional.

The reality was, no-one out there, sitting at home in their armchair pretending to be an expert, knew more than us about that rescue. We had to decide what to do – and have the confidence to follow through with action.

We were here. We knew what the mountain was doing. We knew the challenges. We had the experience and the know-how to get this done, so we should do it without fear.

Early on in the rescue, a whole bunch of ministers and dignitaries showed up to inspect the scene in person. This massive gaggle of people in suits moved around the site chased by journalists, photographers and camera crews. Wi-fi was off – phones were down – there were no comms. When the politicians came, security was heightened.

At the back of the group was a lady. She was so short, you could hardly see her behind this wall of men. She seemed a bit out of place, not in the centre of the action, almost hanging back deliberately.

I noticed this woman did not have a helmet on. The risks to her were real, the consequences quite serious and potentially very dangerous. I knew the whole thing could collapse at any moment. Bits of debris were still falling from the roof of the tunnel. You could get seriously hurt, or worse, at any moment.

I went over to her and signalled at her head. I tried to convey that she needed to wear a helmet. I was worried about her and wanted her to be safe. She shook her head. I was not sure if she simply could not find one, or if she did not want to mess up her lovely hair.

So I took mine off and placed it on her head.

I could see she was really shocked that I would do that. Her eyes lit up. Without being able to verbally understand each other, we connected. We engaged with each other via this fairly simple act.

And I made clear that I cared about her safety – about everyone's safety. I was not going to accept anyone being in danger or, God forbid, anyone getting hurt on my watch.

After that, I stuck with her as the gaggle swarmed through the tunnel. I ushered her ahead of me to allow her to pass through an area before me, so I could follow along and keep her close and safe.

It turned out she was a minister. Word spread about what I had done. It was a pretty simple act on my part, not something I thought meant anything other than basic safety, but it earned me the trust of the project's senior management.

I went to a meeting the next day. There she was, sitting with another senior minister and a representative from the

Prime Minister's Office. It was clear she had told them about me. It had almost qualified me in their eyes.

It meant I could sit at those tables, I could have conversations within the tunnel, and be useful. I could offer suggestions, including advice that was contrary to what had been agreed upon, and be heard. I could offer an alternative and have it considered.

And that is exactly what I would shortly need to do to get those men out alive.

CHAPTER EIGHT

I COULD FEEL IT IN MY WATERS

When I arrived at the rescue site, after visiting the temple and venturing into the tunnel to have my first look at the collapse, I got to meet some of the rescue workers. They were incredibly polite and welcoming, but it was clear that something was wrong.

The mood in the tunnel was extremely flat. Hope was rapidly failing. I thought that if we did not right the ship, if we did not shift this mindset and maintain some kind of optimism, we would doom ourselves to failure.

To help the mission be successful, I felt I had to somehow lift the spirits of everyone involved. I tried to bring a simple and shared purpose. Hope. But I needed everyone on the same page.

I feared that if we did not all truly believe that we could do this, it would turn out the way it almost always does – the tunnellers would die and some of us would probably be killed, too. The whole thing would collapse. It would be a deadly and devastating disaster.

And so, for it to end differently, it had to begin differently. It had to be run differently to how these missions are typically conducted. We simply had to model the outcome we wanted.

Look, I am a pretty upbeat and positive person by nature. I try to see the best in people. I look on the bright side of life when possible. And I always try to hope for the best. But the fact of the matter is that when you are dealing with a disaster, particularly one underground, there are rarely reasons to be hopeful.

In virtually every instance where I have been involved in a rescue, people have died. Either they have died during the initial incident or in the process of a recovery mission.

It is rare – incredibly unusual – for these difficult situations to play out without some kind of fatality. But in India, I was sure we would get those forty-one men out alive. I felt it before I even got out of the helicopter.

We would succeed. There was no doubt in my mind. It was an odd feeling, but it was so strong.

I had to strike the right tone from the beginning. I needed positive and clear messaging, and to put my reputation on the line. That is why I said those famous words to the press pack early on.

'Forty-one men out and safe, all home by Christmas, and no-one else hurt in the process. I promise.'

It was a rigid goal, it is true.

Did I believe it? I think that is too blunt a way of putting it for an answer that is arguably quite oblique.

There could be so many different futures. It would be arrogant to pretend otherwise when dealing with a force as strong and unpredictable as nature. My belief did not come from a place of ignorance, but one of determination. And so I had to focus on the future I wanted to make it come true.

It was by no means a guarantee, but there were multiple possible outcomes. In some strange way, I believed that how I behaved could influence the future we got.

That's my response to the question of just how much I believed in my blunt and bold statement to the press that those forty-one men would not only survive, but be home for Christmas. The scientist engineer in me does not remotely understand this answer, however. He does not comprehend how I have come to land in that position.

To be frank, I am still trying to figure out what was going on inside my head – and really, in my heart and soul – during that unusual time.

I do not know where the optimism and definitive declarations of imminent success came from. They just materialised in my head. It seemed like the right thing to say. It felt like a message I was meant to deliver.

The scientist engineer looks back at that optimism now with dismay.

Of course, some of the armchair experts who initially thought I had gone barking mad now say that everything was always fine, so of course the rescue was a success. They have erased from their memories – and from history – the fact that they believed the situation was dire. They pretend they never accused me of having lost the plot, of being irresponsible and negligent by believing I could save these men.

And the situation was far from fine. I have the data showing that the whole thing was collapsing bit by bit, hour by hour. The challenge we faced was extremely complex.

I mean, the tunnel is now submerged beneath metres of water. The roof caved in further. What does that tell you? What we did was amazing. The extraordinary outcome – forty-one men rescued, home by Christmas, with no-one else hurt – had materialised against the odds.

My forecast on the first day I was onsite felt right. It felt so right. And I think my frame of mind, my determination to bring everyone involved in the rescue on that same journey, kind of worked.

A few months after I got home, I was giving a presentation about the rescue at a conference. Afterwards, a few people who work in corporate communications approached me.

'Who was managing the comms up there?' one asked in horror.

'There was not anyone in charge of communications or media strategy,' I explained. I suppose that was how I found myself cornered by a press pack demanding answers on my first day onsite.

'Who decided you would give that firm promise of forty-one men home by Christmas and no-one else would be hurt?'

'Well, I suppose that was me,' I said. 'No-one told me what to do and what not what to do.'

'Your approach is both awesome and absolutely unacceptable,' one of the public relations gurus laughed. 'It's a textbook example of what not to do in the communications space when dealing with a crisis.'

Broad statements. No specifics. Commit to no-one. That is how things should be done when speaking publicly about a high-stakes situation, especially one where there is plenty to lose.

In hindsight, putting my entire professional experience on the line was a pretty big gamble.

To be fair, however, some of the facts did allow us to be hopeful. No-one was dead, which was unusual. It was a very different scenario from how these things usually go. On top of that, the little air supply line that connected us with the men had not been severed, thankfully, despite plenty of continued movement in the mountain. We could shoot air, food and water to them. We could shout at them to stay in touch.

I had good reason to feel confident. As my nanna would say, I could feel it in my waters.

I was criticised a few times, both during and after the rescue, for appearing to have sought out the press. Some felt as though I was appropriating a very serious situation to get my mug on television. A handful of comments on social media came from people who thought I simply wanted attention, which was why I was speaking to journalists so much.

That definitely was not the case. I never chased the press – for some reason, they liked me and gravitated towards me. I never attended a formal press conference, nor did I call one. I had no prepared remarks. All the interviews I gave, every single time I appeared on camera, came about while I was walking between the site offices and the mountain. It was 100 per cent on the fly.

I think I appealed to the press because I was so optimistic from the get-go. I truly believed we would succeed in rescuing these men and they loved that message. They loved hearing someone with access to the pertinent information speak so clearly and definitively.

It was a breath of fresh air. It was what people across India needed to hear, so I would be pursued throughout the day, every day, by at least a dozen or two dozen members of the media to offer my latest insights on how things were progressing.

Just how much my comments were appearing on television, social media and radio was unknown to me. I had limited access to communications. On top of that, I did not have a whole heap of spare time available to be looking at the news or scrolling through social media.

Sometimes I would get enough phone service to send a text to my wife. Every now and then, she would mention having seen me on the BBC or CNN, which was quite unusual to hear about, I must admit. Occasionally, I would be able to share an update on LinkedIn to members of the association. That was about it.

I had absolutely no appreciation of how many people were watching. I did not know that millions and billions of eyeballs across India, and indeed globally, were glued to the latest information about this incredible challenge we were tackling, which was being covered around the clock in real time via the media.

And a lot of what they were seeing was me. For some reason, I was the one who the media prioritised over the other equally, if not more, capable experts wandering around the site. I suspect it had something to do with me being a white global expert who had rushed to a remote area to help. Whatever the reason, I featured heavily across multiple media outlets for almost two weeks.

And these reporters were ruthless, let me tell you. The saying 'like a dog with a bone' was surely coined about journalists.

They would pounce on me as I was walking to or from the tunnel, and a few times while I was climbing up to the top of the mountain, or down from one.

There is some amusing footage of one poor reporter who was following me, clutching a microphone and gesturing his cameraman to keep up, almost sliding off the side of a narrow dirt path. There was a real chance he could have toppled down a steep embankment, right off the edge of a cliff face. I managed to reach out and grab him by the collar just in time.

'One rescue mission at a time, please,' I laughed.

He did not seem to find the situation very humorous.

Not only was I not seeing these interviews, but I was not getting any 'feedback' about them. I was not seeing the comments. I was blissfully unaware of the growing conversation about me and my efforts. It was not until a while after the rescue that I saw any at all.

When Karl Stefanovic from Channel Nine's *Today* show called me the day after the rescue was complete, I started to get a sense that perhaps I had been featured a little further afield than India.

It was overwhelming and surreal. But at the time, and more so in hindsight, I truly do think it was the right thing to do. It was important to keep spirits up and not allow people to ponder the possibility of failure. Not just on site during the rescue, not just for the workers, and not just for the families of those forty-one men. But for the hundreds of millions of Indians watching at home, and many more around the world, for whom success was absolutely necessary.

We all needed to believe. There needed to be an authoritative but optimistic voice who could rally support for a positive outcome. An outcome that is not often achieved, but which I was sure we could pull off.

But we could only do it if there was not an ounce of doubt, negativity or ill feeling.

There is an earthquake on Day five – it's not too big – some rocks fall inside the tunnel. Is it a warning? A tremor? A precursor to bigger events?

On Day ten loud cracking sounds are heard inside the tunnel near the collapse zone. All personnel are evacuated from the tunnel. It was a sudden, shocking reminder of just how precarious a position we were in. The rescue inside the tunnel is stopped. Everything is stopped.

After reviewing all the data our teams meet. We decide to go back in – we have already lost another day. I am banished from going back in the tunnel again. Naturally I agree and then resume duties underground – of course. I had been told – but I did what I knew I had to do.

CHAPTER NINE

ODD POEMS AND NEW TUNES

Alright, this is where things get weird. Seriously weird. Please bear with me while I try to put into words something that makes zero sense, especially to a scientist.

In the weeks leading up to the tunnel collapse, while I was hatching my plan for a world tour of all things extreme tunnelling, I started to think in poetry. Whenever my mind turned to work of any kind, whether I was preparing for a job or drafting a presentation for a conference of some kind, all my thoughts . . . rhymed.

Ideas rolling around in my head were spontaneously transformed into lyrics that either tumbled out of my mouth or flowed from my brain to my arm, down to my hand, and onto a page or computer screen.

It did not require a great deal of effort either. One day it was simply there. The ability to think poetically.

Much like the trip I was about to go on, it felt almost

impulsive. Something inside of me felt an urge to communicate in poetry.

I have no idea where it came from and I still cannot figure out why it happened. But after reflecting on it in the time since, I think I was simply in a hyper-focused state about my professional world. I was connected to it – all facets of it – in a very deep way.

I mean, I was already pretty obsessed with it before then. I had been since I was a kid, carefully scanning the landscape for interesting-looking rocks. I had devoted most of my life to this stuff. The earth. What comprises it. Humanity's batty obsession with digging into it.

But now, it was like I was mentally linked to it in a way I had never felt. So much so, I thought and communicated about it . . . in poetic form.

Please understand that I am completely aware of how unhinged this sounds. Just talking about it makes me shudder. It is so weird, so totally out of character for me, that I might as well be having an out-of-body experience.

That guy down there sure looks like me. He has my voice and demeanour. And he seems to know his stuff about tunnels. But why is he rhyming about everything like the world's most boring rapper?

There were even a few conferences just before I left on my trip, and right at the start of it, where I presented in poetry. In Cairns, Singapore, Auckland, Munich and Ljubljana. Just picture that for a second. A room full of scientists, geologists, engineers, miners, businesspeople – all the types who might not ordinarily come face-to-face with high-level and pretty straight concepts delivered to them in poetic form.

In Queensland's tropical far north, while speaking at the Australian National Committee on Large Dams conference, I took a crowd through the challenges and opportunities of adaptive risk management when it comes to uncertainty in latent conditions, both in terms of technical and contractual matters.

I would love to see Snoop Dogg work with that kind of sexy material. Can you imagine?

Yet, somehow, for some still-known reason, I kicked off my session at this very niche and serious event by saying:

Damn contracts in our country
In the land of 'one and free'
Tend to be quite complex
Yes, quite complex contracts be.

Have you ever seen a hundred pairs of eyes go totally wide? So wide that the full iris is in view, bordered by white? Let me tell you, it is quite something. I continued:

For in this land of BBQs
Good humour and good mates
It's crucifixion by contract term
When engineers make mistakes.

And on it went for the better part of an hour, before I took questions from the bemused but enthralled audience.

You better believe I gave my answers in totally off-the-cuff rhymes, too.

I could have easily been laughed out of the room but, thankfully, they loved it. Still consumed by rhyming thoughts and concepts, and maybe a little buoyed by the response in Cairns, I did the same thing in Singapore at the Conference of the Associated Research Centers for the Urban Underground Space shortly after. There, while presenting on being adaptive and resilient to the crises of today and enabling humanity's conquest of time and space underground, I observed:

Competitive commercial tendering
Commercial price race to the bottom
Means the variability of the rocks and such uncertainties
Are dismissed and oft forgotten.

And later, in a particularly meaty section about some of the long-term challenges facing our part of the industry, I offered:

It's going to come as a huge shock
Because we think our work is sexy
But many young now turn away
Because they think our work is sketchy.

My LinkedIn lit up with comments from those who witnessed the bizarre but captivating rhyming engineer-lawyer-scientist.

It was a weird state to be in. A few times, I wondered if I was losing it. But it did not feel like I was. On the contrary, it was like my mind was running like the world's best engineered, hand-built racing car.

I was in a completely tuned-in but calm state. Picture a boxer who has trained relentlessly for months and months, sparing no energy and cutting no corners, for the fight of his career. Come the big night, he feels ready. On fire. That was me, minus the physical prowess and blood lust.

I was sharp as a tack and raring to go. It just so happened that everything in my head, and a lot of the stuff coming out of my mouth, was melodic.

At the start of my trip, right around the moment the collapse occurred inside the tunnel high in the Himalayas – which I knew nothing of – I was speaking at an event in Auckland. The Australasian Tunnelling Conference. One of the biggies in my line of work. Exactly the type of event where someone like me suddenly performing poetry might not be well received.

It was, though. Even when I was dealing with some pretty heavy and real-life themes, which happened to be playing out a world away.

The things we design, build, operate and run
Our work 'n' toil – for us quite fun
These things we build sometimes go 'POP!'
Kill a few and hurt a lot.

I had no idea at the time just how poignant those words were, given the disaster unfolding inside the Silkyara Bend–Barkot tunnel. Something had indeed gone POP! in a serious way.

Elsewhere in that presentation, I warned:

Now, here's the thing
My Lesson True
The fear of 'POP!' must NOT rule you
For if it does, I say for sure
Good engineering – it's out the door!

Being crippled by fear. Letting that fear drive you towards rash decisions. Forgetting to lean on your knowledge and trust your instinct. My, how true those ominous lessons would become.

Later, I continued:

For fear of 'POP', it cripples minds
For fear of 'POP', no value finds
For fear of 'POP', deep mindless regulation
For fear of 'POP', engineering stagnation
For fear of 'POP', the fall of nations
Embracing the 'POP', it brings creations.

Right outside the conference venue, celebrations were kicking off to mark the start of the holy Diwali festival. Later that day, my phone would ring for the first time and a chain reaction, months in the making, would finally be set off.

Let me be clear, I have never been inclined to present or speak in rhyme before. I am eclectic and a little unusual, it is true. But not to that extent. I am not the poetry type and certainly not while in a professional setting. Believe me. Honestly, I doubt I have even sat down and written a poem before this strange time.

It just came from left field without warning. It was the last thing I expected to find myself doing.

If all this sounds too absurd, if you cannot possibly believe that I would break out in rhyme while speaking at very serious and proper international conferences, jump on LinkedIn. If you do a search for 'Arnold Dix poetry' or 'Arnold Dix rhyming', you will find countless comments from those who were there.

Something else happened in those months before the rescue when it comes to music. And another major musical shift occurred the moment I set foot on the Himalayas.

Music has always played a big part in my life. I feel like it is a major part of my consciousness. I can hear music playing in my head, on demand. Pretty much anything I want. Not just the lyrics or a few beats, but the entire composition of a song.

My brain is a jukebox and every song I have ever heard is on the catalogue, ready to play at a moment's notice. I cannot think of another way to describe it. I can tap into an infinite palette of combinations of sounds and textures, melodies and rhythms.

Those songs inform, reflect and amplify whatever emotion I am feeling or state of mind I am in. I can use it to self-regulate. If I am feeling angry and want to calm myself, I will put on something that relaxes me. If I am preparing for an exam and I want to feel confident and empowered, I will play something that pumps me up.

I like everything, too. There is not really a genre I do not like. I will listen to anything, so long as it is playing at the right time. In the right circumstance or mood, I suppose.

I will listen to Verdi's *Messa da Requiem*, but I also like the B52's 'Love Shack'. I am also pretty into Mongolian metal rock and I like listening to Russian church choirs singing. I can get lost in absolutely anything.

Music is about more than just entertaining or occupying myself. It serves a far greater purpose than providing background noise. It provides a kind of treasure map to my soul, as soppy as that sounds.

It guides me through a complex maze of emotions, from the highest of highs to the lowest of lows.

When I am feeling off balance or overwhelmed, I can find solace in the way a single melody pulls me out of the fog and into clarity. When I am bored or restless, stumbling upon a new artist or song, or delving into a genre or style that might not normally take my fancy, can get my adrenaline pumping. When celebrating, either with loved ones or on my own, nothing is better than setting a sense of jubilation to a carefully crafted musical score.

And when I feel reflective, I turn to songs from my youth and early adult years, which invoke a whole host of memories, both happy and melancholy.

You know what I mean. Surely, you have days when you wake up and feel like you are trying to swim through a river of mud. Everything feels heavy and hard. There is no spark in your chest or rhythm in your head. It just feels like it is going to be a lethargic slog. Then, you fire up Spotify or the radio, and a powerful drumbeat or arse-kicking chorus tears you from your funk.

In the midst of chaos or joy, contentment or angst, music is the thread that weaves through my experiences, adding colour and depth. It's a companion that dances with me, reflecting my internal landscape and elevating it in ways words can't quite capture.

It is not just discovering new artists and songs that fires me up, or listening to a broad selection of genres, but also figuring out how particular sounds, rhythms and beats are made. Over the years, I have learned how to play the flamenco guitar, the banjo and even the tabla. A tabla is a pair of hand drums originating in India.

Now, as I mentioned earlier, I collect and restore pump organs from the late 1800s. In my house in Monbulk, I have a room filled with my latest completed refurbishments. But the shed is where the real magic – and madness – can be found. About forty pump organs are lying there, waiting to be brought back to life.

If you have never seen a pump organ, it looks a lot like a regular upright piano. The only difference is that you pump pedal levers with your feet that fills the organ's bellows with air. As air travels through brass reeds, it gives you this interesting and almost eerie sound. It would be right at home in a Dracula movie.

They are totally worthless. Truly. Now that I have mentioned it and the picture is in your head, you will start to see them everywhere, I promise. I find mine in hard rubbish collections, on Facebook Marketplace and in junky second-hand stores. They are almost always free. Either I take them, or someone will turn them into kindling.

I think they are beautiful machines. They are quaint and have a lot of charm, speaking to a simpler era. But they are completely useless. No-one wants them, so it is not as though I find myself sitting on some enormous pot of gold.

Music runs through my family's DNA. When I was sixteen, for reasons I still find quite remarkable, unexpected and almost impossible to comprehend, Dad managed to get Mum pregnant. Lo and behold, out of the blue, comes my little sister Helena.

Not long after that, Dad pissed off and left us on our own. Mum had to work hard to keep the home together, so I kind of adopted Helena and became her surrogate father figure. When she was a toddler, I took her to uni with me and would leave her at the campus childcare while I went to lectures.

Early on, it was clear that Helena was a gifted singer. And from the time she was a kid, she spoke about wanting to be an opera singer. This is not one of those careers with plenty of work opportunities going. You cannot really just glide in, be half-good at it and blend into the background. It is a calling for only the very best of the best, and Helena just so happens to be one of those. She is an accomplished singer whose remarkable voice has taken her all over the world.

One of the real highlights of my life, one of my proudest moments as a big brother, was watching her perform at The Met in New York City.

She is the real deal. So much so that a few times now, in media interviews about the tunnel rescue, the journalist has cottoned on to who my famous relative is and the conversation has diverted to Helena. I do not mind that one bit. My beloved little sister is one of the most successful sopranos in the world and perhaps *the* best in Australia. I could not be prouder.

My late brother Colin was quite a character. For all his faults, and there were many, he had a creative and entrepreneurial spirit that led him to some strange pursuits. One of them was producing an album for notorious underworld figure Mark 'Chopper' Read. Yes, that Chopper. And yes, an album.

While behind bars serving a sentence for attempted murder after shooting bikie boss Sidney Michael Collins in the chest, Chopper found himself with plenty of time to think. And he felt those thoughts were best expressed to the world in musical form. A tape recorder was secretly smuggled into Risdon Prison in Hobart. Chopper would find a quiet place to lay down the tracks that would make up *The Smell of Love* by Chopper Read and the Blue Flames.

The Blue Flames was really just Colin, who produced the EP. It was released by small independent label Newmarket Music in 1997. If you find yourself unable to remember any of those songs, do not fret. *The Smell of Love* did not make much of a splash, despite its provocative inclusions like 'The Shower', about the communal prison showers, and 'Hankster the Gangster', detailing a 'very un-nice' foe. But *Rolling Stone* did credit Colin with creating a new genre of music dubbed 'crime grunge'.

Colin also produced and recorded a rap song released by World War II veteran and RSL Victoria president Bruce Ruxton. Bruce was a conservative, outspoken and controversial figure whose public commentary was often racist, homophobic and bigoted. That aside, he was a passionate advocate for issues important to veterans, and fought to restore and save the Shrine of Remembrance in Melbourne.

In a bid to raise funds to support the project's $1.5 million bill, Bruce decided to release a rap single, the 'Ruxton Rap', which was Colin's brainchild. Among the infamous lyrics were references to Paul Keating as a 'Gucci-clad social vulture' and a blunt declaration that 'I like Australia for Australians'. My brother was also the inspiration for an accompanying music video that saw Bruce decked out in a leather jacket and black sunglasses, holding a distinctive boombox.

My cousin Harold is one of Australia's most accomplished Spanish guitarists. He is absolutely phenomenal. As a lover of that instrument, I have been jealous of his far superior abilities more than once. Another cousin, Charles, is a brilliant trumpet player and does that professionally.

So a strong musical ability runs through our family genetics. And even though I only dabble in the instrument side of things, my love of music is incredibly strong.

In the months before the rescue, while I was embarking on this seemingly pointless world tour to explore all things tunnelling, my appetite narrowed sharply. Suddenly, I was only interested in one kind of music.

Essentially, it was anything reflective. Not necessarily chilled, like a Jack Johnson–style playlist that would be perfect to absorb if I was into smoking marijuana. More like music that was a little bit mystical. That was all I could hear and enjoy.

I saved this ultra-relaxing assortment of tunes into a playlist and listened to it constantly while travelling. When I look at that assortment of songs now, I almost do not recognise them. But this was the soundtrack to my unusual state of mind, when I was so in tune with what I was doing, unknowingly preparing for the biggest challenge of my life, this incredible calling of sorts.

The moment I got to the top of the mountain, all interest in music disappeared. Suddenly, I did not want to listen to anything. No matter the flavour, no matter how much I had previously been obsessed with a song, I could not get into it.

More than that – I had an almost visceral physical reaction to hearing music.

I think it was a case of not having any room left in my head for music, or anything really, other than the rescue. I could not find the available space. I was so deeply in the zone, trying to understand everything that was going on, that other rhythms, melodies or emotions had no chance of competing.

That was very unusual for me. Normally, I listen to music all the time. In the shower in the morning, in the car driving, at night while cooking dinner. Music is a constant, even if at times only in my head. Now there was none. I listened only to the mountain. For this task, the focus I needed to have meant there was no space for music in my mind. I've never experienced that before.

CHAPTER TEN

FORTY-ONE KIDS

As I left home in Australia to begin my global tunnelling journey, it was dawn and still dark outside. I picked up my daughter's work boots by mistake. Unable to see and still tired from my alarm going off so early, I was sure they were mine. And so I had no choice but to wear those boots each day during the rescue mission in India.

They did not fit me. By quite a bit. After the first day, I had a couple of painful blisters. By the end of the operation, they had absolutely destroyed my feet. But every step I took in Hannah's boots, in and out of the tunnel, up and down the mountain, to and from meetings, was a reminder of her.

It was a reminder that my own child regularly ventures into similarly dangerous spaces to the one these forty-one young men had. And so it wasn't about my discomfort and the few lasting scars resulting from it, but about getting those kids out alive.

During those weeks, I would think of Hannah often. I would recall holding that tiny bundle in my arms when she was born, bouncing her on my knee when she was a bright and bubbly toddler, and introducing her to the world of tunnels when she was in primary school.

My mind wandered to the woman she is now. Confident, fascinated by the world, always up for an adventure. I pictured her wearing these boots as she walked through tunnels deep beneath the earth. Once or twice, my thoughts ventured to uncomfortable places – like how I would feel if, God forbid, something happened while she was underground.

I would do anything to get her out. I would wear small and tight boots until my feet fell off if it meant rescuing her. I would be anxious, fearful and deeply distraught, just like the families of those forty-one men, some of whom had gathered outside the tunnel site.

Hannah's boots kept me grounded. They kept my mind laser-focused on the task at hand – getting those other kids out and home safely to their loved ones.

Of course, I did not make my thoughts known to my kids or my wife Divina. I maintained a level of positivity, and mostly kept them in the dark about how serious things were and just how involved I was.

The text messages I managed to send back home when reception permitted were deliberately vague about what I was up to. They were also sprinkled with just enough emotion to remind Divina and my kids that I loved them, without sparking panic that I was prepared for the worst.

'Honey, I'm sitting here in an office staring at a whiteboard,' I told Divina on a rare phone call one afternoon. 'Don't worry. I'm completely safe.'

Several hours later, a news report with vision from the rescue site that day – from inside the tunnel – captured me with a team of engineers. It was as clear as day. I was right at the pile of debris that separated the forty-one men from the outside world. Bar a hardhat, there was nothing to protect me from serious injury or death if another catastrophe occurred.

I was sprung. The jig was up. Divina knew I was far away from the safety of a makeshift office.

'I have to be,' I tried to reassure her. 'I have to get these kids home.'

Once upon a time, probably not that long ago, there might have been less fanfare in India about a rescue mission like this. The workers, the men who go far from home in search of work and a meagre income for their families, are low caste or even lower, to the point where they are not part of the social hierarchy at all.

So in the past, there might not have been much concern about their wellbeing. A few decades ago, there certainly would not have been around-the-clock media coverage and genuine care and empathy for the men's wellbeing in a time of crisis shared among hundreds of millions of people.

But in this case, Indians cared. They cared a lot. Virtually the entire country was united in shock and concern, but also in hope for a positive outcome. I wonder if it was because the country has changed and continues to change – transforming at a rapid pace, it should be said – as its economy booms.

Since ancient times, probably somewhere around 1500 BC, Indian society has operated under a social hierarchy known as the caste system. Its history, how the caste system has played out and the deep, still-present ramifications on social development and inclusion in modern India are complex.

At its core, the caste system divided people into different groups called varnas, based on their family history, historical occupation and general standing. The Brahmins were the priests and scholars who dominated and influenced just about everything. The Kshatriyas were rulers and warriors who held the wealth and political, military and diplomatic power. The Vaishyas were wealthy and successful landowners and merchants who fuelled commerce. And the Shudras were labourers and other workers, everything from doctors to builders.

Outside of the four varnas was a much-maligned group called the Dalits, the so-called 'untouchables'. Overwhelmingly, they were excluded, abused and discriminated against, often to a severe extent.

India's caste system prevailed for a staggering 3500 years because of its origins in sacred texts called Vedas. The oldest scriptures in the Hindu faith, the Vedas, were composed in Vedic Sanskrit and set out much of the basis for how society should be organised. They outlined a careful hierarchical structure and, over time, these ideas became more rigid.

Castes were largely hereditary. Unlike other established societies, there were few, if any, opportunities to claw your way up the social ladder in traditional Indian society.

You inherited your status and that is largely how things remained for generations. Those born into a caste stayed there. For life.

Your position in the caste system would dictate virtually every aspect of your life – who you could marry, what jobs you could do and even where you could live.

Religious and cultural norms meant that the caste system was reinforced and deeply embedded over thousands of years, right through to modern times.

The original purpose of the caste system was to create social harmony and maintain order. In reality, it has been criticised as leading to a concentration of wealth and privilege among the elite, and significant, widespread inequality and discrimination among the poorest. Those in the lower castes, and especially the 'untouchables', were destined to live difficult, if not unbearable, lives, performing menial jobs for a pittance.

Things have obviously changed over the past century, but not entirely, and incredibly slowly. India's independence in 1947 signified a turning point. The country's constitution, written three years later, made it unlawful to discriminate on the basis of caste. The derogatory term 'Dalit' was replaced with 'scheduled castes', and a range of policies, including affirmative action principles, followed in a bid to uplift impoverished and marginalised sections of the population.

Despite legal advancements, particularly in the areas of discrimination and equality, as well as a recent shift in social attitudes among younger Indians, the legacy of the caste system is still evident in India.

This is especially the case outside the major cities in rural areas, where low-caste and scheduled caste Indians still face challenges and discrimination. In urban communities, however, it appears the caste system's influence has waned dramatically. For the most part, people are treated fairly with a focus on merit and equality.

In recent decades, India's economic and social development has seen a gradual shift away from caste-based discrimination. Education, urbanisation and economic growth have been significant drivers in changing attitudes. Like so many advancements, younger people are also playing a big part. Especially in the cities, young people largely want no part of a country where the caste system is tolerated. They reject that level of prejudice and are not afraid to say so.

India is on a journey of transition. Tradition and modernity are increasingly in conflict, often in complex ways, but on the matter of caste, it seems as though progressive thinking will prevail.

People are being treated better and better. Even the poorest and lowest ranking ones are now considered by broader society.

I'm lucky to have been able to be a part of a special time in history for India.

CHAPTER ELEVEN

THE RIGHT THING TO DO

I knew exactly who those men trapped in the tunnel were. I had never met them, I did not know their names at the beginning, and there was a significant language and cultural barrier between us – as well as tonnes of rock and twisted metal and concrete – yet I knew them.

It's because I had seen them – or men just like them, more accurately – in Qatar. So many of them.

Young men in their late teens or early twenties who came from really poor parts of India in search of a way to support their families. They wanted to work. They were happy to work. If they wind up somewhere they are paid ten bucks a day, they will probably be thrilled. But they will send nine dollars of that pay packet home to their families.

They're desperate. They're determined. They're selfless.

They will do whatever they need to, go wherever their legs will take them, and work as hard as they can until their backs are almost breaking. They will not complain or ask for more, and typically they have got the biggest and brightest smiles on their faces because they feel like they are doing something big and something important.

They are providing for the people they love, hundreds or thousands of kilometres away.

Working underground is an extremely dangerous job. I have said it before and I will say it countless times over the remainder of my life – humans are not meant to be there. And yet, underground is the setting for so many of the aspirations of society in the twenty-first century.

From poor young men travelling to faraway lands to work in tunnels and mines in support of their struggling families, to mammoth nation-building projects that are offering benefits for future generations yet to be born. From deep metal mining to exploring the essence of time and space with humanity's most sensitive instruments, deep underground.

Once upon a time, Qatar aspired to host the FIFA World Cup. To get the country ready, and show the world that their Middle Eastern kingdom was a mighty and advanced one, the country required tens of thousands of men.

They ventured from Indian, Pakistan, Nepal, Bangladesh and all corners of the African continent.

My specialty is making infrastructure work, especially complicated underground infrastructure, and definitely when things are not going quite right. But I also have expertise in fire safety management, among other technical engineering requirements. I have a reputation for being able to pick up a problem and run with it.

Brief me, I'll come in and train your workforce, I'll get machines to work in ways they are not meant to, I'll find a way through when there does not seem to be one. I am Mister Fix-It. That's not to sound arrogant, but is how I have come to be regarded around the world over the past three decades.

I think what has appealed to many who have hired me is that I also have a reputation for being able to do those things, and more, without making a song and a dance.

I would come in quietly, do the job, then disappear again. Few people, if any, would know I was ever there.

That is what Qatar was meant to be. But it was a bloody mess.

One of my jobs was to train a couple of thousand people to run Qatar's new airports and tunnels. While I was doing that, I started to notice worrying things happening with a lot of the men.

They were falling asleep. In huge numbers, too.

I could not figure out why so many of these workers were literally sleeping on the job with no qualms. They weren't even trying to hide it. They would just stop where they were, drop what they were doing and get some shut-eye.

Push came to shove. I was fed up. I had to figure out what the hell was going on. It did not take long until I discovered the horrid truth.

They were not going to sleep. They were starving.

The shocking extent of their hunger was such that they were slipping in and out of consciousness. So many of these migrant workers had been imported into Qatar with little to no regard for their wellbeing. There were no arrangements for these men when they lobbed into Doha. They were swallowed by a massive system and had to fight to survive, all while working hard around the clock for fairly meagre salaries.

I had stumbled upon systemic worker abuse without looking for it, the likes of which I had never witnessed before. The scale was so enormous, it beggared belief. Even in the darkest recesses of my mind, I could not have pictured a worse situation.

I'm hesitant to use the word 'slavery'. It was close to it, though.

In the press were infamous portrayals of thousands, if not tens of thousands, of people being worked to death. There were instances of that, for sure. But the broader issue was far more complicated than that.

A perfect storm of unfortunate factors saw desperate and aspirational men from the poorest parts of the world lured to a land of promise. It saw ultra-wealthy royals and politicians, blinded by a determination to prove their prowess to the world, rubber-stamp huge expenditures with little oversight. It saw opportunist and immoral conmen slink from the shadows to make their fortune at any cost.

You had this huge number of young men who had left their homes and families to venture into the unknown to make something of themselves. They had not sought personal glory or wealth, or aspired for greatness in a way that you and I might know it. They were sacrificing so much, especially their health and their lives, for the people they loved.

Almost everything they made in this brutal existence in Qatar, they sent back home to those they had left behind.

Knowing all this, a number of people in Qatar realised that they could capitalise on it and make a lot of money.

A system was established where migrant employment agencies offered the opportunity to connect aspiring workers with unbelievably exciting and lucrative opportunities in Qatar. For a fee, naturally.

Essentially, they sold people a pathway to a job in Doha. An elaborate and lucrative trade was created with human beings as the product. And it was worth a mammoth amount of money, which these greedy and ruthless monsters raked in.

Some unwitting workers bought visas that did not exist. Other people were promised jobs that never materialised once they arrived in the country. Still more signed up for one job then discovered it was something entirely different.

Those job opportunities were unbelievable because they were not real. For countless men who paid their life savings for a chance that could change their and their families' lives, the work simply did not exist.

They arrived and found . . . nothing. This meant a lot of people were immediately in breach of whatever conditions they had agreed to when they entered the country. This made them extremely vulnerable and prone to abuse.

It was a disaster. And so many workers were starving as a result.

I couldn't turn my back on the situation. I couldn't avert my gaze and pretend I had not seen these horrors with my own eyes. I was working with these suffering men at an enormous scale. Thousands of them. I had to help.

I drained my bank accounts of almost every cent. I sold all my investment properties. I assembled the biggest war chest I possibly could.

Then I established Qatar's worst-run company. I ran it for eight years before hitting the self-destruct button and returning to Australia. It lost an eye-watering amount of money, but it enriched – and saved – the lives of thousands of people.

I came up with the idea of establishing a company that I ran really badly, which could justify me staying in Qatar well beyond the scope of my initial project. The company could quietly buy huge volumes of essentials, help people with visas and, ultimately, get people out of the country when they wanted to leave but were otherwise stuck.

We organised medical assistance for people who were injured or ill. We arranged work for people. We rescued women from forced sex slavery. Some of those workers had few options after arriving to a mountain of broken promises, a situation that was seized upon by those looking to exploit the vulnerable. Many women, and also some men, were driven into sex work.

They would be collected at the airport and quickly realise there was no beauty parlour or hotel. It was usually explained to them that the business had not opened yet but it would soon. In the meantime, accommodation had been arranged. They would go to a house and live with a dozen other women.

While there, being 'supported' by someone and not earning an income, they would have to find a way to pay rent.

'But I don't have a job,' they might say.

'That's not our concern – you must pay,' they would be told.

Usually, the suggestion would be made that they could do sex work temporarily to earn some money and pay their way. But just for a while – just until the beauty parlour or hotel opened.

The alternative? The women would be reported to the authorities for breaching the conditions of their visa. They would be arrested, charged and deported.

By this point, they had probably paid a few thousand dollars for the 'services' of their migration agent. I heard instances where women had paid $10,000 for a 'visa'. That is a huge amount of money in any context, but particularly for those from developing countries. It was hard to say 'no'. The idea of leaving so abruptly, not just empty handed but thousands of dollars in the red, was not something many could fathom.

That's how it was. So many were desperate to escape this awful situation. And so we helped them flee.

We even got people out of prison who had been arrested for some minor reason or on trumped-up charges.

I would hear a case of someone being behind bars for something unjust. A visa breach. Stealing a bit of food.

Sometimes even just 'loitering' in a well-to-do neighbourhood while being poor and the wrong shade of brown. I would drive up to the prison, tell the guards that I needed some workers, then identify someone who I knew was qualified.

If I said it with enough authority, they would agree and release this bloke to me. It was vital that those in charge of major projects for the World Cup, which Qatar had pinned so much on, had whatever they needed to get the job done.

But the most important work this company secretly oversaw was an underground soup kitchen of sorts. People who were starving, who had no options and few reasons for hope, were fed without knowing where the food came from.

I would also support Qatari households if they extended a bit of help to those in need. In a nutshell, I created a network of safe houses on a mammoth scale.

It was all done without anyone knowing.

We operated on different days. I did not want the authorities to notice any kind of pattern – the bulk purchase of products, the movement of pick-up trucks, the appearance of strangers in a neighbourhood – that might draw their suspicions.

A major component of our work was distributing food in bulk. To the workers who were starving, of course, but also to locals who were down on their luck.

All you had to do was take in one or two people in need, workers who were 'irregulars' or those in spots of bother, and the company would provide you with some kind of assistance. A bit of money. Plenty of food. Healthcare and medicines. Whatever it was.

I was still doing real, actual work for much of the time I was in Qatar. I was inspecting fire and evacuation safety systems at stadiums. I was working on the underground metro. I was helping at the airport.

Our company employed lots of people. Legitimately. And by overseeing that hiring process, I ensured those workers were paid properly, treated well and not exploited.

At one point I even became the *Guinness World Records* tunnel verifier in Qatar. I trained teams of inspectors to audit and verify Qatar's world record attempt for having the most tunnel-boring machines running at the same time. I was the extreme engineering judge and verifier for that record attempt.

But the real purpose of the company was to ensure the continued running of this large-scale, unofficial humanitarian program without anyone knowing. But it was haemorrhaging money. To keep things going, I had to make some big sacrifices at home.

Earlier in my life, I had done what a lot of Australians of my vintage did and invested in property. The path many of us took, or believed we had to take, was to buy a family home then use it to propel us into being landlords.

I had one in Sydney, right in the inner city in Chippendale, and one in Melbourne's west. I sold both of them. I did quite well, given I'd had them for so long and they were in good areas.

I funnelled the money into this company so I could continue running the support network. That injection of funds, which robbed my nest egg, meant we could carry on what we were doing in Qatar for eight years.

We helped thousands of people.

In mid-2023, I was in Washington, DC for work and had posted something on LinkedIn about why I was there. Almost instantly, I got a message from a man named Waheed, one of the workers who I had helped in Qatar.

'Let's have lunch!' he suggested.

We sat down to eat with plenty to catch up on. I asked how long he had been living in DC. It turned out he was not a local at all. He had seen my LinkedIn post, reached out then hopped on a plane from Los Angeles.

That's a long way to travel for a burger.

And so, in a quiet corner of the vast lobby of the Hilton Hotel, we sat and caught up on life.

Waheed is a Nigerian man who was a geologist working with the World Health Organization before he found his way to Qatar. Part of his job was to help with drilling wells to supply clean water and sanitation. He'd drilled more than 123 wells in his time there.

He made some money, built a house and was on his way to having a good life when he heard about Qatar and the World Cup. There was an opportunity for him to go to work there.

He was approached by a 'migration agent' who offered the world – if he could pay 1 million naira, which at the time was roughly A$8000. That's an enormous amount of money in Nigeria.

The job was working in oil and gas. It sounded very exciting. He was told that his salary would be about US$10,000 a month. It was extraordinary. He would pay his visa back in no time with this executive-level position. And he would be able to fundamentally alter the course of his family members' lives.

He sold his house and packed his bags. He bought a plane ticket. Then Waheed found out, all of a sudden, the visa fee had doubled. Of course it had.

Waheed was picked up from the airport in Doha and taken to a house. He had been promised comfortable accommodation that he could rent for a reasonable price. Instead, he was led to a regular-sized bedroom with fifteen people sleeping in it. He had to pay to sleep on the floor. The whole place was infested with bed bugs. All over the walls was blood from where the men would pick them off their beds and squash them to death.

His entire life was packed into one small bag that he slept with. He had a single cooking pot tied to it.

Waheed felt distraught. It had all been a lie. Nothing he had dreamed of was ever going to materialise.

On that first day in Qatar, he went to a mosque to pray. He began to cry. He felt like he could not go home – he had invested everything he owned to be there. There was no going back. The shame of failing and having to face his family, his community, felt far too great.

He was desperate to survive. Most days, Waheed walked to the bus station to travel to construction sites – any site he could get to – to beg for work. But no-one really wanted workers. There were more than plenty. Most companies had arrangements with these dodgy migration agents. So more often than not, he would be chased off by armed security guards.

Getting food was impossible. So men like Waheed did not really eat. If someone managed to get their hands on some form of sustenance, like a few cups of rice, the fifteen men would share it. If they were lucky, they would eat once every few days.

One morning, he was in the house and someone received a telephone call. There was a job site that needed workers – an airport project that had just got underway. Waheed told everyone in the room, who he described as his brothers, and they all rushed to the site.

They got hired, but the salary was a stipend. It was better than nothing, but not by much.

Waheed began working on a section of Hamad International Airport, now considered to be one of the best in the world. That is where I met him.

'I have to thank God for you,' he told me on that emotional day in Washington, DC.

After I met Waheed at the airport, I took him into my crew as a safety officer. I trained him up and helped him to find other job opportunities. I assisted him and those living with him with regular food.

The food would come in the night so the neighbours did not see. No-one really knew where it was coming from. Waheed suspected it might have been me.

That food, that life-giving sustenance, removed a lot of the desperation those people felt. It took many people off the streets, meaning they did not have to beg or steal.

Waheed recalled his roommates remarking: 'Where is this coming from? Is it from heaven? This is like magic.'

When he decided to get out of Qatar, Waheed applied to study an Associate's Degree in occupational health and safety technology in the USA, in Seattle, Washington. He was accepted. After he graduated, he got an internship with a massive tech company and, after that, secured a full-time role.

He has since worked with Facebook, Microsoft and Amazon. He worked for a company that recycled cars to manufacture reused steel. Now, he's in the aerospace sector working for Blue Origin, the space company founded by billionaire Amazon founder Jeff Bezos. He is literally helping to make rocket ships.

In Washington, DC that day, he told me that I had made a huge impact. I changed the way he viewed the world. I was the first white man who had ever related with him in a way that transcended race. He told me that I treated him and his 'brothers' like humans. Something so simple for me, something so enormous for him.

Who is this man? he thought when we first met.

As he ate a chicken sandwich and I tore into my medium-rare burger, we spoke about the decade that had passed since we met in those extraordinary circumstances. We spoke about what it means to be human, to act with grace and to be kind.

'The brotherhood is not in the skin. The brotherhood is not in religion. It's in people like you,' he said. 'That's what it means to me.'

'But you see,' I replied, tears welling in my eyes, 'to me, it's in you.'

Who would have thought a decade ago that we would be in this situation? I was bursting with pride. I was so happy to see how wonderfully he was doing, and how happy and secure he was.

And he is now paying it forward in the USA. He is coaching and mentoring young people who need help with their professional development. He is working with immigrants, particularly young Africans, in pursuing their professional dreams. He is passionate about supporting people who are vulnerable and need a bit of support.

'This is what we need from humans,' he said.

I couldn't agree more.

That's the essence of human decency. Full stop. It's not about skin colour, it's not about religion, it's about finding unity in caring for each other.

Since the India rescue, I have heard from more and more people who I met during that time in Qatar. When I was in the news, they had seen me again after all these years, after not expecting they would for the rest of their lives. It is so incredible to see where they have ended up and how their lives have turned out.

*

I am not going to lie. Running this clandestine operation was terrifying. I knew that if I was discovered, if the perpetrators cottoned on to what I was doing, it would not go down well. Not many, if any, people in positions of power would see it as a positive thing. I would probably cause a great deal of embarrassment and unwanted negative attention.

Honestly, I might have ended up in jail. That did not sit well with me. Arnold Dix isn't really built for prison.

But I also knew that if I did not do it, no-one else would. I could help. I was crazy enough to help. So I did.

For especially difficult cases, for those who wanted to get out of the country but were trapped for whatever reason, I would hatch an escape plan. Usually, it was an almost absurd idea that I could not make happen on my own. I would need help from someone with means.

I began socialising at various embassies across the city. I don't know if you have ever been to a function at an embassy or ambassador's residence before, but it's quite an experience. There are soirees of some variety every week or so, with all the trappings you would expect of a high-level event. Diplomats from other countries would come to meet their counterparts, network and informally discuss any issues that might be on the agenda.

I would go along, meet people who might be able to help me and try to gently facilitate an exit via a friendly country.

Any country that assisted would deny ever knowing me. And that is how I expected things to be. It was off the books, it was non-sanctioned, and that is how it had to be to help those who desperately needed an exit strategy.

A lot of people chose to ignore what they were seeing. I could see these desperately poor people, who had been lured to this rich country with the promise of a better life, now starving in the street. The suffering and injustice were evident. But for so many foreigners just like me who were in Qatar, it was too painful or helping would have presented too much of a risk, so they looked the other way.

Money has a way of blinding angels.

I teamed up with an academic named Professor Ray Jureidini, an expert in migration ethics at the Islamic School of Ethics. He is also an Australian scholar. I became his eyes and ears for what was really happening in the gutter.

There was also a judge who became aware that I was a sympathetic figure. He would refer some of the difficult cases before him to me and I would offer pro bono legal advice and guidance to these people who could not afford a lawyer.

It was a very difficult time. Many parts of that eight-year experience were traumatic. A lot of it now sits uncomfortably with me – witnessing up close what happens when the worst of humanity, the facilitation of mass exploitation, is allowed to fester.

It was like living in a horror movie at times, only the monsters had human faces and forms.

I was glad when it all ended. The last person I helped get out of the country was a Chinese woman who was in a precarious position. She had been used and abused, and wound up in prison countless times. Through my embassy networks, I was able to facilitate a quiet escape via an Eastern European nation.

The moment I knew she was out, that she was safe, I got on a plane. I have never been back.

During that time and in the years since, it must be said, Qatar has seen a whole range of reforms. Things are markedly different from how they were. There has been an overhaul in how workers are treated, the migration system, construction regulations, and more. From what I hear, things are better now.

In some ways, I think if I hadn't had that enormous and deeply impactful experience in Qatar, I might not have connected so emotionally with the rescue operation in India.

Qatar humbled me in a way I never would have imagined. It made me appreciate my privilege. It opened my eyes to the power of privilege – the opportunity to use it for something good and to make a difference.

Qatar opened my eyes to how so many people in the world view work. For so many, it is not some sort of ambition, like it was for me. It is not an exciting or rewarding undertaking. It is a means of survival – for them and for so many half a globe away who rely on them.

That is how the tunnel project in India felt to me. Poor young men, desperate for an opportunity, for a chance, working in dangerous conditions, who had run into trouble.

It was not just forty-one workers who were trapped. I linked each of them to the people they were helping back at home, to those they loved and who loved them back, for whom working in that tunnel was already a matter of life and death because it funded their survival.

Calculating that out, and at least a thousand people were on the other side of that rock.

CHAPTER TWELVE

A MINOR DOPAMINE ADDICTION

I am a bit of a dopamine junkie, I have to admit. Like all successful addicts, I have somehow managed to construct an environment where there's no shortage of supply of the good stuff I crave.

Luckily, I do not have to try very hard to find an adventure. Adventures tend to come quite easily to me – and at great frequency. They are always exciting jobs, which makes virtually every invitation irresistible.

Generally, the phone will ring in the afternoon from a company or government that has run into an issue of some kind underground. I will get a rundown of what has gone wrong and how critical the situation is. If it is urgent – and it usually is – I can be on a late flight that evening or first thing the next morning. I usually meet with the client less than a day later. Depending on where they are, of course. I offer a 48-hour service anywhere on, or should I say under, the earth!

Some of these requests can be challenging to navigate, depending on where the crisis is. The Australian authorities do not love the idea of people travelling to certain counties. And some underground activities tend to make security officials nervous.

Think eastern and radiation.

These jobs demand quirky itineraries – no simple online bookings. And the boarding passes will definitely be flagged by border security officials.

I suppose a silver lining of suddenly being 'known' since the India rescue is that bureaucrats in many Canberras of the world are, hopefully, no longer reading my urgent emails seeking clearance to go to country X for the purposes of tunnel Y, wondering if I am some kind of spy. Or a maniac. Now, I'm Arnold the underground tunnel guy and, on most measures, a pretty safe bet.

For all of 2023, I was probably only home in Australia for two months in total. At the most. It is not uncommon for me to go off somewhere and just not come back for a long while. It is too expensive to go in and out, in and out, and the flights to and from Australia are a real punishment with most places I travel. So a lot of the time, I just set up shop somewhere.

I have got to say, though, I am feeling a bit tired at the moment. India really took it out of me, more than any other job I have done. I am feeling puffed in a way I am not used to.

I wonder if this is what being an old bloke is meant to feel like?

'Well, it was hardly a holiday,' my wife said, when I mentioned this feeling to her recently. 'You could have been killed.'

I guess she has a point.

I have always been quite private about what I do. One reason is that existing in the shadows suits many of my clients. Something would go wrong, I would sneak in, fix it, then disappear again. Secrecy was a good thing; it ensured my pipeline of work kept trickling.

But another reason is that this line of work is kind of weird to talk about with strangers who are not in this world.

For example, if I was at a dinner party or backyard barbeque with someone talking about their fantastic family holiday to Bali, where dad had a wild ride on the back of a moped, that makes for a perfectly fine story. I have nothing against Bali or mopeds.

But if someone then asked me about the scariest moments in my work, when I was underground or off God knows where doing God knows what, then suddenly old mate's Bali yarn is blown out of the water.

'Probably the assassination attempt in Albania,' I might reply. Like a clichéd scene from an old Western film, the music might stop with every eyeball in the place turning its focus on me.

'Attempts, I should say. They had three goes at killing me in the end.'

*

To understand why there were not one, but three attempts on my life while I was working on a tunnel job in Albania, you need to understand what state the former communist country was in at the time.

Throughout the 1990s, Albania was a powder keg. Political corruption and a growing sense of authoritarianism were forcing the population to the brink and, by 1997, civil unrest had swept through the country.

A series of government 'investment' deals, more on par with Ponzi or pyramid schemes, collapsed in quick succession. Billions of dollars of public funds were lost. In all corners of Albania, furious citizens took to the streets. Daily demonstrations and fierce fighting saw an estimated 2000 people killed over an eight-month period.

Attempts at a peaceful transfer of power from the incumbent and now-collapsed Democratic Party government to the reformist opposition party were unsuccessful. Restoring order to the country seemed impossible. People were simply too angry at what had been allowed to transpire for years.

Rebel fighters seized control of southern Albania. It looked as though other major centres could also fall. The military, ordered to squash the civil unrest, was both fatigued and overwhelmingly corrupt, so its leadership largely ignored the commands. Foreign countries began evacuating their citizens and a United Nations Security Council resolution was hurriedly passed, seeing several thousand NATO troops deployed. Other countries, including the USA, assisted in a peacekeeping operation.

International pressure saw Albania's political class agree to an interim reconciliation government, with national elections held shortly after. The Socialist Party swept to power, defeating the Democratic Party.

Sali Berisha, a heart surgeon turned career politician, had been the president for five-odd years until he and the government were turfed out in 1997. Incredibly, he returned to a position of power in 2005 when he led a coalition of five centre-right political parties to victory at the national election. He became prime minister.

But it was not an overwhelming victory, so Berisha and his allies knew the government had to take big and bold steps to convince the people they were worthy of remaining in power. Their strategy included building a series of major infrastructure projects that would deliver economic growth and employment opportunities.

One of them was Albania's first-ever tunnel highway, in the Tirana region in the country's northwest. The almost five-and-a-half kilometre twin tunnels were part of a mammoth highway project spanning some sixty kilometres. The tunnels helped to slash five hours off the travel time from Tirana, Albania's capital, to the Kosovo border.

In the lead-up to the 2009 election, things were not going well. The project operators had underestimated the scope of works and the challenging ground conditions. The whole thing was besieged by delays and a major budget blowout. Initially expected to cost about 375 million euros, it was almost triple that estimate.

I was called in at the eleventh hour to help ensure the tunnel could open, and open safely, before the election the prime minister was determined to win.

At some point in 2008, Gail and I arrived in Kukës, a semi-rural area in the mountains about a thirty-minute drive from the tunnel site. We were put up in the Amerika Hotel, this absurdly opulent pile beloved by Russian mobsters and drug dealers, who would sneak into Albania to wash their dirty money.

The place looked like the set of a James Bond movie – swathes of marble, everything gold-plated, an unnecessary number of crystal chandeliers – but everything was a tad tarnished around the edges.

It was totally out of place. At the time, Kukës was technically a city but felt more like a country town. Partially built roads, a few dusty town squares and not a whole lot for locals to do. There was so little in the way of amenities that the residents' favourite pastime was to walk the loop of the town over and over again. You would see men meandering down the street with hands clasped behind their backs, their wives several steps behind them.

Kukës was a very poor part of Albania. To travel east from the bright and picturesque Mediterranean part of the country to the border with Kosovo was a bleak experience. The transition from affluent and beautiful to impoverished and on the verge of destruction came without warning.

In Kukës was a single restaurant, but it was not really what you might imagine a restaurant to be. It was simply a public place you could go to eat. There were two large rooms connected by a doorway, no menu or any semblance of choice, and fairly gruff hospitality. You would be told what was available and then pay for it.

One night, Gail and I went to try the local delicacies, whatever they might be that evening. A small colour television set sat in the corner of the room playing the evening news. A story came up about the discovery of a mass grave. Everyone stopped what they were doing, stood in solidarity and began to cry. It was an incredible display of public shared grief, which gave a stark insight into how much this country was still hurting.

The place had an eerie feel. I can't quite describe it, but a darkness hung over Kukës when we were there. People would peer at us out of the corner of their eyes. When men looked at Gail, they would almost grimace, as though pained by her mere presence.

It was so unsettling that the two of us came up with a special code, a certain knocking pattern, so she knew whether or not to open her hotel room door.

After all, the tunnel project wasn't popular locally and, as a result, people were very suspicious of us.

One of the most important issues in struggling places like post-revolution Albania is employment. If you cannot work, you don't have any money. If you haven't got any money, you can't feed and house your family. Without those basics, you are understandably going to be pretty pissed off at those in positions of power.

Men in the local town had found jobs during the construction phase of the tunnel. But by the time we got there, the actual building process was coming to an end, so those opportunities had wound down and dried up.

I think everyone accepted that as a natural part of the process – the digging was done.

But then a pink man with a weird accent arrived. Within days, he had employed fifty men and started training them to be the operational crew to run the tunnel when it opened.

None of those men were locals, it turned out. That was a major problem – a major problem for me.

I did not know any of that, of course. The Prime Minister's Office gave me a list of names of men I should hire. I did not know those men. I had no clue they were from elsewhere. I suppose someone in a political position thought they were spreading economic love by giving long-term jobs to men from a different district.

But because I was an outsider and my arrival coincided with the beginning of a new phase of hiring arrangements, I was seen as the reason.

Naturally, a bunch of angry local men decided to kill me.

They got really close, too. A seething mob got within a few metres of me when a bus screeched to a halt behind me. Its door was flung open, and I was dragged inside and whisked away to safety.

This did not seem to be an unusual occurrence in this town and on this project. Rumours suggested that, earlier on, one or two other senior people involved in the construction phase had died in brutal circumstances. I am not sure what their crimes were, but the whispers made clear that those deaths were not carried out with guns. It was much nastier than that.

The assassins used metal bars, wooden bats, chains and just about anything else heavy they could get their hands on to bash their targets to death. That day out on site, I was meant to suffer a similar fate.

Gail was standing right next to me as the mob ran towards us. She thrust herself between me and them. But she did not get dragged into the bus that rescued me. In the rush and panic, I didn't realise that Gail was left standing there. I was terrified something was going to happen to her.

My rescuer explained that it would be culturally frowned upon for those men to harm a woman – a foreign woman, at that – and so she was probably going to be fine. In the moment, it was fairly small comfort. Thankfully, my rescuer was right.

We decided not to go to work the next day. Later that evening, we discovered the bus scheduled to take me, Gail and our team from the hotel to the tunnel site had been hijacked.

Gail and I took that bus each morning. A mob had forced it off the road and jumped on board. They were looking for me. They were still determined to kill me.

We received a phone call to check why we hadn't showed up at the site. It was the Prime Minister's Office. This was a major nation-building project after all, so it was being monitored at the highest level.

When we explained what had happened, the authorities quickly swung into action.

Special Forces police swooped in. They watched us like hawks. We were guarded closely. I was taught a special hand signal that I could flash if I was in trouble, so my protectors could swoop in. A search began for those who were responsible.

The authorities did not have to look very far. A few days later, the group of men – I assume it was the same cohort – appeared at the entrance of the tunnel site looking for me, unaware that we had protection. I made the sign, and the waiting Special Forces police nabbed them and whisked them away.

I thought that was that, until those enormous military killing machines returned to my hotel a week later with three beaten and bloodied men.

I remember it so clearly now. It almost seems laughable, albeit terrifying. It was breakfast time and I was about to have something to eat. One by one, each of the men was presented to me. They apologised and asked for forgiveness. Based on the loose translation I was given, they even promised not to try and kill me again.

'You have a choice,' one of the officers said. 'You can accept the apology and we will release them. Or you can not accept, and . . .'

And what? As his voice trailed off, the silent void it left hung longer and longer in the air. Then the answer dawned on me.

Holy shit. 'And we kill them' was the likely end of that sentence. If I wanted to, I could shake my head and this trio would be dragged off to God knows where and executed. I got the impression that, in this part of the world, apologies are perhaps not accepted that often.

They were shaking uncontrollably. The look of desperation

in their eyes was unnerving. I felt a heavy sense of sadness wash over me.

'I accept their apology,' I replied.

I am not sure they understood my words, because I doubt they spoke English, but my body language and the gentle tone of my voice obviously said enough. The men let out a collective sigh of relief. A gasp really. They had probably been holding their breath for the minute or so it took me to realise what was going on.

'But could you ask them not to do it again?'

They didn't. It was made clear that I had no real say over hiring decisions. I was merely there to do one job – my job. I assume they went back to their neighbourhoods and passed on the message. I lived to tunnel another day.

It also helped that they saw I had some really tough guys on my side – they weren't going to succeed in offing me without suffering some serious bloodshed.

That entire experience was a strange one for me. And not really because I was in the crosshairs. It was deeper than that.

I have always been a pacifist. I abhor violence. But in that moment, when the angry mob was racing towards me with metal bars and bits of wood in their hands, I was faced with a split-second choice.

Before that bus sped up and saved me, before I knew there was any hope of an escape, I could see I was probably going to die. A seemingly inescapable fate confronted me.

Would I fight back? *Could* I fight back? Having to make that decision – to potentially kill someone in defence of myself – was sickening to think of after the fact.

I could have. If I had the means, I would have killed them. I had been pushed right to the limits of my morality at rapid speed and, having time to think about it, I instinctively landed on 'fight for your life'.

I am just as big a barbarian as anyone else. I am not smarter and more well-rounded, I don't possess some special quality that means I'm not a wild animal somewhere deep inside. If I had to do it, I could do something unspeakable. I'm a barbarian, too.

It made me realise that we shouldn't necessarily be surprised when someone kills another human being. Instead, we should be determined to ensure no-one is ever put in a position where they need – or want – to.

Death has always fascinated me. Not the scary movie type – not even the macabre. My interest, or I suppose the place my mind wanders to, is in the injustice of it all.

Not just how randomly and often unfairly death seems to come, but because modern societies grant licences to inflict it on ourselves and others.

For the most part, we are not allowed to administer death lawfully. It does not matter how worthy the recipient might be in your eyes, either tinged with love or death, you cannot take a life.

Although, the lawyer in me is tempted to whisper: 'It depends.'

Killing is often acceptable in acts of self-defence. Say you are protecting your children from an intruder. Or a policeman is confronted by a knife-wielding criminal.

We train scores of men and women to become killing machines and send them abroad to take lives beneath our flag.

But what about an otherwise normal person who kills in a way that is deemed unlawful or unjust? How they are then treated intrigues me.

It is not quite as simple as you might think. It is a subject that people far smarter and more philosophical than I am have pondered for centuries.

Take this example. Every single time you get in your car, you must slide a seatbelt across yourself and securely fasten it. If you decide not to and a cop catches you, you can expect a mammoth fine and the loss of several demerit points.

Why? For your safety and the safety of others. Not using a seatbelt dramatically increases the risk of you killing yourself and others, should something go wrong. Even if that accident is not your fault, even if the only thing you did wrong was not put on your seatbelt, you would still have some element of blame.

But why do we allow people to climb onto the back of a motorcycle? That vehicle is devoid of any of the protection like a car's shell and airbags, which are carefully engineered and produced to offer the highest possible level of safety. Motorcycles obviously do not carry seatbelts. They are incredibly dangerous and reckless.

How might society view someone who comes off their bike and dies? Or someone who collides with a pedestrian, someone on a bicycle or another motorcyclist, with the loss of life occurring as a result?

Perhaps not so bleakly as the motorist who failed to put on a seatbelt. After all, the motorbike rider has fulfilled their obligations to the established social contract. Sure, they caused death – theirs or someone else's – but they did what was expected.

It might seem like I am going down a rabbit hole, but for engineers and scientists, this is serious business.

I have had a long career responding to disasters, investigating what happened and, more often than not, analysing death. In a way, I am the Grim Reaper's detective, playing my part in the great blame game of death.

How the taking of a life, whether one's own or someone else's, is viewed and judged makes a difference when it comes to the design of just about everything. Not just the design but sometimes how an item or concept is imagined.

Do you think health regulators would approve the production, sale and consumption of alcohol if someone invented it tomorrow? I highly doubt it.

Even though death is inevitable, how death is judged and the consequences for causing it can vary, depending on the time, location and circumstances. I find that interesting.

All of that aside, I believe death by another person's intentional hand will only encourage more death, whether it is a state-sanctioned execution in Texas or a madman's knife rampage in London. An eye for an eye, or a tooth for a tooth. It is in our DNA as a species. As we see every day, both here in Australia and in places we probably could not find on a map, death is too often doled out indiscriminately by humans.

The only solution is to save life. To cherish it. To celebrate it in all its forms. To step up and protect it when the opportunity arises.

To do otherwise just propels us deeper into a cycle of hatred and more death.

CHAPTER THIRTEEN

CURIOSITY COULD HAVE KILLED THIS CAT

For much of primary school, I was a pretty average learner. I was so behind academically that I was considered to be a remedial student and placed in the lowest classes.

My mum, concerned about why I was underperforming to such an extent, agreed to the school's request for me to sit an aptitude test.

'Arnold, how can this be?' the principal asked, after calling me into his office when the results came back. 'You should actually be in the top class. How did we not notice this?'

I did not know. Until that point, I guess I had not really been told there was a possibility I could be smart. For most of my schooling, I was unfocused, unchallenged and probably a bit bored.

And given how often my family moved, uprooting me and delivering me to a brand-new school with its own take on the curriculum, it was hard to settle into a rhythm of learning.

My education had no consistency. Whenever I would lob at a new school, I had no clue which way the teacher wanted me to do division, and whether it should be long or short. I did not know how I should write. When I had a question, I did not know whether I should raise my hand or stand up. Should I use a pen or a pencil? I had yet to get my pen licence, which was a real thing in the olden days.

It was different in every place. The first few times, just as I had grasped how things were meant to be, we would move again. So I stopped giving a shit. Then I got shoved in the remedial class.

No-one noticed that I was not meant to be there, although I probably did not give them many reasons to reconsider. That is the way things had always been, so I leaned into the expectation that I was merely below average intelligence. I never thought to challenge it. I kept my racing mind, full of ideas and bursting with imagination, to myself.

I was thinking about plenty, too. I would daydream about different possible designs for perpetual energy machines. One of them was basically an alternative form of hydroelectricity using a pistoned plug instead of a turbine. Another involved using lasers that might be able to get a spaceship to travel at the speed of light.

As a little kid who was disengaged at school and a bit of a loner, because making friends was hardly worth the effort when you were destined to be uprooted, this is the sort of stuff I would think about. Rockets. Energy. Atomic particles.

Mum put her foot down with Dad. She was determined that I should get a better education. A consistent one, where

I could be in the same place, learn and make something of myself. She was so pissed off about it that she essentially threatened Dad. Spend money on a good school or she would stop working. He could run the hotels on his own.

From the middle of Grade 6 until the end of high school, I went to the Haileybury School in Melbourne.

It probably took me all those years to get up to speed. I was pretty behind by that point. But I wound up on the Honours Board, much to the horror of some of the teachers. I was not well liked by a few of them because I was always up to no good. Not bad in your conventional sense. Not a bully or a thug. Just a little bit mischievous.

The science teachers loved me, though. They could see my clear passion and determination to learn everything I could. In my final few years, they would let me teach some classes on exothermic reactions in chemistry to the kids in my year.

Anything that went boom, I was your man.

I was a master of building the best bombs and rockets. Back in the good old days, before terrorism was a thing, you could get your hands on a whole heap of ingredients to make explosives relatively easily.

Ah, the good old days, when kids were free to potentially lose a few fingers, maybe even a whole hand, by building a bomb in their backyard.

I am not talking about your amateur, run-of-the-mill soda rocket either. I mean the kind of rocket that rattles windows and sets off every dog in a three-kilometre radius. The kind of rocket that has the neighbours coming out of their house, certain they are about to see the aftermath of a major car accident.

Of course, today's lack of access to explosive materials is a good thing. Being a kid with a wild imagination and the means to do something about it comes with some obvious risks.

I electrocuted myself a few times. Really well, too. I was fascinated by this invisible thing that powered everything around me and I wanted to explore it. I was very lucky that young people tend not to die when they are hit with a really big shock. It just makes their heart beat really fast for a while. And when you are a kid, that is pretty exciting.

I would pull stuff apart. Before I knew about electrical insulators, I would use any old screwdriver (sometimes even a butter knife from the kitchen drawer), whack it into a machine and open it up.

I do not recommend that kind of approach for children. Or people of any age, really.

I had one of those Tandy Electronics kits that I would play with for hours. I used it to completely take apart a train set my parents got me for Christmas one year. Rather than be content with the locomotive and carriages gently going around the tracks, I got stuck in with my kit in a bid to make it voice-activated.

It did not really work, but I had fun trying. I just liked to experiment and see what would happen. A true, budding scientist. And I never really minded failing.

*

The world holds an inherent fascination for me. All parts of it, too. My range of interests is not limited by subject. My mind is ticking over, wondering how something works or racing with observations about someone I have just met.

Even as a kid, I had an ability to suck up information. I did not come from a massively educated family or anything like that, so we did not have a library at home.

We did own the Childcraft encyclopedias, however, and I read every single one of them from cover to cover. I read the Bible, too, but mostly for the rude and gory bits in the Old Testament. My grandfather gave me the complete works of Shakespeare, which was very cool, given to him at the age of thirteen and given to me when I became a teenager too.

Other than that, I would usually come across something, find it interesting and absorb everything I could about it.

Some of the stuff that grabs me and gets my mind going is a little out there, I will admit. Take the Paris Museum of Sewers, for example.

Most people who travel to the French capital choose to spend their time doing what is considered to be 'normal' tourist stuff. Taking in world-class galleries, absorbing the work of some of history's greatest artists. Sitting beneath the red awning of a classic café or bistro at noon or in the early evening, sipping on a café au lait or a glass of syrah while watching the city's famously fashionable residents wander by. Lazily cruising along the River Seine beneath the shadow of the Eiffel Tower.

Not me.

That stuff all sounds fine, but on one of my last visits to Paris, I spent several captivating hours in the bowels of the city at the Museum of Sewers.

If you are ever so inclined, you will find it beneath the Esplanade Habib-Bourguiba, near the Pont de l'Alma in the seventh arrondissement. Here, visitors are welcome to learn all there is to know about the history of the city's sewer tunnels.

Hugues Aubriot, a fourteenth-century provost, was responsible for overseeing the development of some pretty formidable sites of significance, such as the Bastille. He also built the first sewers in Paris in the late 1300s.

Museum visitors receive a fantastic introduction to the brilliant, complex and persecuted Aubriot. He was a visionary with a sharp mind and a focus on the future, helping to lay the foundations – quite literally – for modern Paris. He was also a bit of a rebel, angering the powerful church with his progressive views and favouring of science over faith.

After the death of King Charles V, with whom he was exceptionally close, chaos gripped Paris. Simmering tensions began to boil over and Parisians came to blows, with the city's Jewish population copping a lot of hatred and discrimination. Aubriot was incensed by this and ordered the arrest of those found to have harassed Jews.

The church was furious, ordering him to stand trial on several false or embellished charges. Among them, heresy, extortion and even sodomy. He was sentenced and faced certain execution, if not for his friendship with a lauded noble who intervened, saving his life.

Instead, Aubriot was handed an arguably worse fate – life behind bars, within the Bastille that he helped create, with nothing but bread and water to sustain him. As luck would have it, later civil unrest in Paris saw a mob swarm the Bastille and release a bunch of prisoners, Aubriot among them.

He quickly and quietly slipped out of the city, but hundreds of years later, his legacy remains, even if he is not a household name.

Let the hordes have the Louvre, the Centre Pompidou and the Musée d'Orsay. The Museum of Sewers is where the real action is. Live demonstrations, fascinating insights into the advancements in practices and technologies over centuries, the chance to explore a deep labyrinth of tunnels. What a day out!

Although I have been to the Louvre, it must be said. Many times. But I bypass the usual favoured pieces like the *Mona Lisa*, *The Coronation of Napoleon* and *Liberty Leading the People*. Even *Venus de Milo* cannot distract me, even though her spectacular marble came from the ground.

No, I head somewhere very special. Somewhere most of the crowd probably skips. In a room on the ground floor of the Richelieu wing, you will find the Code of Hammurabi, created in ancient Babylon sometime between 1792 BC and 1750 BC. The two-and-a-quarter-metre tall obelisk contains the laws of Babylon that were developed during its earliest days, carved into black diorite.

As an engineer, it is a sight to behold, imagining how it might have served a function as part of the design of the Temple of Marduk. As a geologist, the beauty of the stone and intricacy of the carvings are breathtaking. As a lawyer, it is fascinating to see such strong parallels with the customs of thousands of years ago and the moral principles underpinning society today.

This legal text was recorded towards the end of the forty-year reign of Hammurabi in Babylon's first dynasty. They are a collection of 282 of his sentences, covering everything from trade tariffs and marriage and divorce to crimes like theft and murder. The ideals displayed were incredibly advanced for the time.

Carved deep into the surface of that rock, among many other lawyerly matters, are details of the consequences faced by early scientists, builders, engineers and physicians who cause death.

For instance, if a builder makes a house for someone and its construction is shonky, and it collapses and kills the owner, then the builder must be put to death.

In an interesting twist, however, if the shonky house causes the death of the owner's son, then the builder's son shall die. And if the collapse kills the owner's slave, then the builder must give him a new one.

Well, I said it was progressive *for the time*.

Anyway, you can see why this particular museum artefact might capture my imagination. At some point, I got it into my head that I would love to trace the origin of the obelisk – the source stone onto which the Code of Hammurabi is carved.

The Louvre is a little hesitant about anyone handling their exhibits, which I suppose is fair. They are also known to resist working with experts who are not French. Rightly or wrongly, they prefer to prioritise giving access and sharing expertise with their countrymen and women. I guess I can understand that level of preferential treatment from such a renowned cultural institution, and the pride of Paris.

So I figured it might be quicker to head to Oman for some field work. I identified a few locations where there could be ancient quarries, Sohar and Wadi al Jizzi. It was here that I determined black diorite might have been mined many, many moons ago.

Working with an Omani geologist I had befriended, Dr Mohammed Alkindi, we would take samples and conduct testing to understand its characteristics. Should it match the Code of Hammurabi in the Louvre – if the authorities allowed us to compare and contrast – then the implications would be enormous.

This finding would demonstrate that Oman played a key role in the ancient civilised world, and offer a possible physical location for some of the places referenced in ancient texts. It would change how we think about human history's first civilised societies, with Oman at the centre of the transition from the ancient world to the modern one.

I was planning to travel to Oman in 2020 until a little thing called Covid threw a spanner in the works, cancelling my trip and putting the idea on the backburner. That was a disappointing blow.

Because travel was impossible, I lost all my international work. I had one active contract in Saudi Arabia with a team on the ground, testing new fire safety systems in an underground railway in Riyadh. I could supervise their work remotely, so that job ticked along in the background. But apart from that, I had nothing.

In an instant, my wings were clipped. My livelihood and source of adventure – of adrenaline and spirit-sustaining energy – disappeared overnight.

Just before the pandemic had been declared – a time of chaos and madness – my opera singer sister and I said our goodbyes. She was in an isolation room in a bleak London hospital, her lungs haemorrhaging from Covid. She lived – only just – and now sings again. But Long Covid has cursed her.

My stepdaughter Trisha was living in the Philippines. As the death toll started to mount, we got her a tourist visa and booked her a flight to come to Australia. I suggested to Divina that we fly to the Philippines and retrieve her, but we delayed. And so Trisha was confined in a small house in the Philippines for the years of the Covid lockdowns.

Melbourne might boldly claim the longest lockdown, but hundreds of millions of children had it worse than the entitled could imagine. Children were locked inside – no school, no playing outside – essentially under house arrest.

There was no way I was going to sit inside the house and twiddle my thumbs for months while we were in lockdown – or years, as it turned out. I had to do something to keep myself busy.

So I started producing podcasts. It was fun for a while. My sound studio was my wardrobe (not a fancy walk-in one, but an old-school wardrobe in which you might find a lion and a witch). I recorded them in my pyjamas, wrapped in my doona.

A job was going at Nishiki Nursery in Monbulk, not far down the road from my lonely rural sanctuary, for a truck driver to deliver plants to customers. That sounded pretty cool, so I thought I would try my chances. I have been investigating fatal truck crashes for decades (my style of side hustle) and I enjoyed the world of trucks and truck drivers.

If I took up something like truck-driving, I figured, I could meet and interact with new and interesting people – from a distance, of course – which is something most others in Victoria had now been forbidden to do.

I could get out on the open road, windows down and fresh air belting my face – yet another luxury now deemed impossible, at least more than five kilometres from your home. I could use my hands and keep my body active.

I looked at my resume for the first time in a long time – all fifty pages of it – and promptly took a knife to it. Who would hire a barrister and scientist to drive a truck? The assumption of those reading it might be that I had suffered some kind of midlife crisis.

That was easily fixed – I just removed everything after Year 12 and added all my occupational and vocational training:

- Truck licence (heavy articulated)
- Vermin and pest control (Agricultural Chemical User Permit (ACUP))
- Sodium fluoroacetate (1080) chemical endorsement

- Para-aminopropiophenone (PAPP) endorsement
- Firearms (pest and vermin control)
- Hairdressing (not completed).

I was set. I was now a self-employed farmer looking for some extra coin, and off I went.

Nishiki Nursery gave me my first break – dealing with weeds, not driving trucks. I set up a weed-control program and secured my first contract. This activity expanded quickly as local farmers discovered I was a handy weed exterminator.

Soon, Nishiki had me on standby as their first reserve truck driver, and driver Peter took me under his wing and showed me the runs. All of Melbourne was in my range and some of rural Victoria, too.

I became part of the team: a reliable truck driver and weed sprayer.

One afternoon, Divina and I were seated outside Monbulk Fish and Chips in our high-vis truck-driving clothes after a hard day's work when Chippy from Nishiki Nursery bounded over.

'You won't believe it!' he declared. 'There's a guy on TV who looks just like you! He's the spitting image – he's talking tunnel disasters.'

How about that? A guy who looks just like me, with my name, on TV! Divina and I said nothing. For sure we would tune in we said, and thanked him.

Around the same time, my donkeys started getting killed. I thought it was wild dogs and I asked the Shire of Yarra

Ranges Council for help. They sent Dave, their environmental 'adjustor'. That was how my career in vermin control began.

Dave is special. He can form a meaningful sentence just by combining facial gestures and hand movements with 'F' and 'C' words.

He's a boxer – a prize fighter – bare-fisted and now a bit broken after a motorbike crash. And importantly for my job, he is a crack shot with a rifle, like no one I have ever known. Proudly Aboriginal, Dave's single mother taught him traditional hunting to survive in the bush. His also consumed by conspiracy stories from Fakebook.

As Dave and I ridded the world of rabbits, fox and deer by stealth on those long Covid nights, we became immediate friends.

Dave is convinced I am Aboriginal by descent. He says I 'hunt like a blackfella' because I tread softly, love the night, gain no joy from killing, celebrate softly and have no fear in the dark. Auntie Louise Peller agrees. She thinks my mob are from up north because I'm a wanderer.

Dave and I are a classic 'odd couple', who adjust the number of vermin and pests that are destroying the habitats of the helmeted honeyeater and platypus in the glorious remnant temperate rainforests east of Melbourne. As we work, we talk ancient civilisations, aliens and all shit Fakebook through the glorious nights. Dave's Fs and Cs are complemented by my slippery barrister's tongue. People who meet us are always confused by the union.

An emergency nurse, Dave's wife Raelene is the sweetest woman. She lovingly calls him 'skank' and has done so since their childhood when he used to run off with everyone else's girlfriends. Dave makes her feel loved and safe – he takes no prisoners – and she likes that. Dave is a teetotaller – she likes that too.

When Dave realised I was down on my luck during the Covid lockdowns, he asked me to do pest control with him. He gave me a thermal night-vision scope (the sort you see in combat computer games) and helped me set up my business to feed my family.

When I protested at the enormity of the gift, he explained (using C and F words with gestures and hand movements) that he would smash the scope with a hammer if I didn't accept it politely. Dave can be persuasive.

Why would I share these Covid stories and friendships here? It is because good people are everywhere. They are all around you. Decent, generous, wonderful humans are the majority, who are hidden right in front of your eyes.

Humans are mostly like Chippy, who did not see that the truck-driving Arnold sitting outside Monbulk Fish and Chips was actually Arnold from the TV who helps people in tunnels. And people like Dave – the tough, gruff contract shooter and boxer with the heart so big – are around you now. They are in the supermarket, driving cars, on the train – they are us.

To see good, you must open your eyes – you'll even find good in the mirror if you look hard.

And sometimes, to achieve a greater goal, good people need to lie. At the rescue site, I lied by omission. When I made my promise, I never mentioned that I've never saved anyone before – but I like to think I'm still a good person.

I have lived in Monbulk for about thirty years. Back then, our house was a dingy little cottage on a chunk of land and not much else. But I slowly built up the house, making it into a warm and inviting space.

Even though we are so close to Melbourne, no-one here feels a need to venture in. Most other regional areas in Victoria are determined to make themselves into a mini-city. They want to be grown up and sophisticated, just like Melbourne.

Monbulk is not like that. It is quite content being a genuine farming town. It has never been hung up on trying to be something it is not. I think not being on the tourist trail helps. No-one comes here unless they live here or are lost, really.

A lot of immigrants arrived in Monbulk after World War II and that influence is still present. Lots of Italian and Dutch people, who set up little farms. The local shops still stock weird liquorice from the Netherlands as a result.

Those who live here tend to work here, too. You either own a farm, work on a farm, or work in a job that supports farming. You are unlikely to find suit-wearing professionals who commute to the city. It is just not that kind of place. It has stayed largely intact the whole time I have lived here. There is something nice about that.

The biggest thing to happen in Monbulk was when Aldi came to town about five years back. That was a huge deal.

It was at that very Aldi store that I bought my cheap high-visibility workwear, which I wore each day in India during the rescue.

Melbourne, and that busy and frantic kind of life, feels a million miles away. Everyone in Monbulk knows each other and gets along. We have a Facebook group for my little neighbourhood where we keep in touch. We have a barbecue every year, each taking turns to host festivities. We have a radio channel so if there's a bushfire or something else serious, everyone knows to turn to channel 4.

We look out for each other. The sense of community is strong. It does not matter who you are, if you are a decent person and not a dickhead, you will be just fine.

My property is about forty acres. It is not a real farm, although it is probably meant to be. I grow beans and flowers. I have pet donkeys and emus that run around and keep the grass under control. That is about it.

Even though I have been here for so long and know the locals pretty well, no-one had any idea what I did professionally until the tunnel rescue. Suddenly, I was everywhere. The secret was out. They had long assumed I was just an unsuccessful flower farmer who somehow made enough of a living, against the odds, to stay alive.

I love flowers. The best ones we produce here are sunflowers. Tall, fat ones that are seriously beautiful. We have tried dahlias of late, but they have not worked out very well, so I suspect we will stick with sunflowers.

Some years we have good crops, other years it is very ordinary and we fail spectacularly at making any kind of money. I reckon the best year by far was the one when we used pet food. Seriously. We had bought a bunch of commercial sunflower seeds and they had not germinated. I was really pissed off because it cost a fair chunk of coin. Then at the supermarket one day, I stumbled upon bird food filled with mostly sunflower seeds.

I wonder what would happen . . . I thought to myself. Before I could finish the thought, the bag was in the trolley and I was on my way home.

Divina and I did a germination test in the kitchen, using soaking wet cotton wool and some seeds. It worked beautifully. I could hardly believe it. I went back and cleared out the shop of every bag of bird food and we planted it. And by planted, I mean we threw it on the ground and watered it. We ended up with a massive crop – our best result ever. How about that?

About fifteen years ago, I started work on creating my pride and joy. My very own Stonehenge. While travelling the world, I had come across and been amazed by a lot of ancient buildings and architecture that was linked to major events. Kings. Gods. Tumultuous times and celebrations.

A lot of monuments were built with the sun and its position in mind. They signify the winter solstice, summer solstice, equinoxes, and so on. I find that kind of cool. There is something a bit mystical about it, combining the human with the natural in the form of celebrating the sun.

It just so happens that from my house, I have a beautiful view to the east. I can see the full stretch of the horizon. At sunrise, it is a pretty spectacular sight to behold. I decided to build a birthday machine out of rock. Big chunks of rock. In essence, it commemorates the birthdays of people I love.

I set about designing the placement of rocks to fall directly in front of the sun at the start of a new day on a particular date. On my mum's birthday, for example, the big orange and yellow orb gently rises from behind the stone I selected for her. I sit on a bench in the perfect spot and mark her birthday in my own unique way.

When I started working on this monument, I tried to be really clever about it. I did mathematical calculations to figure out how I was going to position all these stones. I did some computer modelling in a bid to make it easier. I really overthought the whole process. In the end, I just sat down and watched the sun rise on the day I wanted to celebrate.

That process took me a few years, figuring out the exact movement of the sun throughout the seasons, including the winter and summer solstices. Then it took me a while to source stones for the people I wanted to acknowledge in some way.

Currently, there are ten rocks in place. I will continue adding to it over time. When I place a stone for someone, I encourage them to come and carve whatever they want on it. It is their rock, so they can make it their own. Naturally, my boys carved penis caricatures into theirs. Dix = Dicks. They thought it was hilarious.

The funny thing is that stonemasons have been doing the same thing for thousands of years. You can see small hints of it in ancient Egypt. My boys thought they were being really funny and clever, when in reality, they were just carrying on a famed tradition. But they certainly left their mark, I suppose.

I love the sunrise. I think it captures the essence of what makes me tick, in that I am inherently optimistic. I love the promise of a new day. I like that the slate from yesterday is wiped clean and you get to have another crack.

And each day is totally different. How much cloud cover there is, or whether there is none at all, the time of year, the length of the grass and what shade of green it is, the weather – they all play a part in making each sunrise unique. Like snowflakes, no two sunrises are the same.

CHAPTER FOURTEEN

ARE YOU THERE, GOD?

In my university days, I spent time exploring various world religions, alongside other lofty interests (like philosophy and spirituality) that many in their first year or two of an academic pursuit indulge in.

I am a scientist first. I am interested in things I can see, touch and experience, and things I can measure and prove. Or at least see proof of. I have a respect for spirituality and certainly would never judge anyone for having – or not having – faith.

But I was and remain fascinated by religion. And so I undertook a kind of intellectual quest using the same rigorous, analytical mindset that I applied to my scientific studies.

My foray into world religions began with the question: what drives humanity to seek meaning beyond the physical realm?

As a student obsessed with empirical research and the quest for objective truths, I was intrigued by the subjective and deeply personal nature of religious belief. I took classes on comparative religions and philosophy, eager to understand how different cultures grapple with questions of existence, morality and the divine. I read books on the subject. I spent time talking to people from all kinds of religions.

One of the most striking aspects is the sheer diversity of religious beliefs and practices across the globe. Each religion presents a unique lens through which its adherents view the world, offering a rich kaleidoscope of stories, rituals and philosophies.

I delved into the major world religions – including Christianity, Islam, Hinduism, Buddhism and Judaism – as well as lesser-known traditions such as Zoroastrianism, Shintoism, Sufism and various Indigenous spiritual practices.

When exploring Christianity, I was captivated by the emphasis on love, forgiveness and redemption. In the newer parts of the Bible, at least. The teachings of Jesus Christ, particularly the Sermon on the Mount, underscore a radical approach to interpersonal relationships and morality.

Concepts such as 'turning the other cheek' and 'loving one's neighbour as oneself' offered a powerful counterpoint to the often transactional nature of human interactions.

I find it intriguing how these teachings have influenced Western ethical frameworks and social norms. It also exposes how supposedly Christian nations have a tendency to warp the teachings of Christ, ignoring them to serve their own needs.

Hello, USA. I might be talking about you right now.

My studies on Islam revealed a religion deeply rooted in the concepts of monotheism and submission to the will of Allah. The Quran, with its poetic and intricate verses, presented a vision of a just and compassionate God, who is intimately involved in the world's affairs.

Particularly moving is the concept of ummah: the sense of global brotherhood and solidarity among Muslims. The practices of Ramadan and Hajj also showcase the discipline and devotion embedded in Islamic spirituality.

Hinduism, with its rich collection of deities and philosophical diversity, offered me a complex and multi-faceted view of spirituality. The ideas of karma, dharma and moksha intrigued me because they propose a framework for understanding human suffering and the pursuit of liberation.

The *Bhagavad Gita*, a central text in Hindu philosophy, provided me with profound insights into the nature of duty, righteousness and the self. The notion of the self as a reflection of the divine was thought-provoking.

The Four Noble Truths and the Eightfold Path of Buddhism presented me with a practical approach to dealing with suffering and achieving enlightenment. The concepts of non-attachment and the pursuit of Nirvana show a way of understanding human desires and the nature of reality.

The practice of mindfulness and meditation in Buddhism resonated with my scientific understanding of the mind's ability to influence wellbeing.

Judaism's rich tradition of ethical monotheism and its covenantal relationship with God gave me a compelling perspective on morality and community. The Hebrew Bible's stories of struggle, justice and faithfulness illustrated the resilience and adaptability of the Jewish people. The practice of mitzvot, or commandments, and the emphasis on social justice and compassion in Judaism highlighted the role of ethical living in spiritual practice. Parts of that really spoke to me.

Each religion has its own elements but also shares a lot of similarities with the others.

A central theme across all religions is humans' quest for meaning. Whether through the divine, the natural world or personal relationships, religious teachings consistently reflect a deep-seated desire to understand our place in the cosmos.

Many religious traditions also emphasise humanity's interconnectedness. Concepts such as compassion, empathy and solidarity are common threads in teachings from various faiths. This interconnectedness is mirrored in our scientific understanding of ecosystems and the interdependence of living organisms.

Recognising our shared humanity can foster a sense of global responsibility and ethical conduct. I have always believed that. But after the rescue, I feel it now more than ever.

Practices such as meditation in Buddhism, prayer in Christianity and Islam, and contemplation in Hinduism underscore the importance of self-reflection and mindfulness. These practices, which enhance mental wellbeing and self-awareness, align with a wealth of scientific findings on the benefits of mindfulness and stress management.

Religious teachings frequently address moral and ethical behaviour, offering guidelines for how to live a virtuous life. Various traditions emphasise concepts such as justice, mercy and integrity. These ethical principles often align with secular moral philosophies and can inform our understanding of social justice and ethical conduct in a broader context.

Even if you are not religious, even if you have no real interest in the notion of faith, I think understanding these important structures can be useful. Ultimately, so much of religion comes back to having empathy, living ethically and pursuing knowledge.

As well as religion, I have a deep appreciation for philosophy. I am a huge fan of Epicurean philosophy, which emerged around 300 BC. What draws me in is how Epicurus recognised the vital importance of pleasure, friendship, justice and music, while also warning of the dangers of politics. I'm fascinated by his concept of an infinite universe with endless realities, and his belief in not fearing God or death. His ethics, his logic and his quest for knowledge all resonate with me deeply.

These values are central to both my professional and personal lives. I hold them central to science and just the goal of being a decent person.

When I kneeled at that Hindu temple each day during the rescue, the images of that pretty simple show of respect sparked chatter among some of my colleagues in the world of science. They thought I was being foolish. I was behaving inappropriately, it seemed, and some were extremely offended by it.

We are scientists. We are searchers of rational truth. Why was I behaving as though I suddenly believed in gods and spirits?

But why would I *not* bow down at a temple in such an awe-inspiring place? What was the alternative? Arnold Dix versus the Himalayas? I would not stand a chance. I had to show respect to and some kind of harmony with the mountain. It felt right to me. I urged others to do it too, but they scoffed.

If being a bit thankful to a god for the uniquely lucky position we were in could be worthwhile, even just showing the Hindu rescuers that I respected them and their beliefs, then who was I to object?

We didn't have a disaster. No-one was dead. We were in the middle of an epic – an ancient epic. How did this huge collapse occur without anyone being killed? That never happens.

It struck me that the universe was still undecided about what to do with these forty-one men. That is how Hindus saw the situation in any case. So I was happy to join them in giving thanks and humbly asking for the situation to remain that way while we worked to get those kids out and home.

In hindsight, bowing at the temple the moment I arrived at the rescue site could be one of the most important things I did during the entire course of the rescue.

It showed the workers who had been toiling away for days and were feeling deflated that I was not just some big, pink Western man coming to take over and bully them. I was one of them, for a while at least, for the time we were to spend together trying to save these men.

I cared. I wanted to understand and learn. I was there to help.

The Indian press responded strongly to the level of respect I showed to the Hindu faith. My kneeling at the temple each day was viewed as a sign of my humility. It almost confirmed my commitment to this enormous task and my faith that we could get it done.

I was acknowledging the power of the mountain and the frailty of human life. By bowing down to the gods, I was showing that I recognised my position.

Not all my attempts at showing respect to the gods were successful. One day, after sliding around on top of the mountain for most of the morning, I went back down and prepared to enter the tunnel. I made my way over to the shrine to kneel down and offer a prayer.

This worker came rushing up and, unable to speak English, gestured wildly at my back. It turns out I had torn the arse out of my pants. If he had not stopped me, I would have gone up to the temple, got down on my knees, and flashed my backside to dozens of journalists and camera crews, as well as hundreds of millions of people watching on.

Some of the army guys had to lend me part of their kits as my small amount of clothing began to deteriorate. There is a photo of me dressed head-to-toe in a fetching white outfit. I look like a doctor, or maybe a ghost, but it is the standard issue camouflage gear for military operations conducted in the snow.

The more I read about the Hindu goddess Kali, the more she made sense to me. I felt I understood her because of so many of the difficult, tragic and destructive things I had seen throughout my career. Her rage, her love, her devotion to renewal. I felt like I had encountered Kali countless times.

In my career, I have found a lot of death. My view of untimely or unplanned death is that it is fundamentally unfair. A lot of the time, it feels like a fate that is unequally distributed, often mercilessly, by someone who is in a bad mood.

Kali is an imposing figure, to say the least. Her skin is a vivid shade of royal blue, or sometimes black, depending on the depiction. She has wild, piercing eyes and a bright red lolling tongue.

She wears a distinctive skirt threaded with human arms and an eye-catching necklace made of severed heads. Kali is usually depicted clutching various weapons in her multiple arms, and often a man's severed head.

It perhaps goes without saying, but she is the Hindu goddess of death, doomsday and time. She is complex and powerful, as much about fearsome destruction as she is about natural transformation.

Derived from Sanskrit, the name *Kali* means 'she who is death'. She is an inevitability – she will devour all in time. Kali searches for evil, ignorance and ego. She is also irresistibly attractive to mortals, over whom she wields ultimate power and control.

While the associations with violence are pretty clear, Hindus also see her as something of a mother figure and a beacon of material love. That is because Kali embodies the essence of shakti, or feminine energy, fertility and creation.

Kali's significance extends beyond mythological tales. Hindus believe she represents the raw power inherent in the universe, which both creates and destroys. She is often regarded as the personification of Shakti, the primordial feminine energy that underpins the universe. In Hindu cosmology, she is seen as the consort of Shiva, the god of destruction, with whom she balances creation and dissolution.

Yes, she destroys, but not indiscriminately. Hindus believe Kali ultimately clears a path for growth and evolution.

She is widely worshipped, especially in India's eastern region. Among many, she is revered as the Divine Mother. Rituals carried out in her honour seek to receive the gift of spiritual expansion, protection and liberation.

One popular narrative recounts her emergence during a battle between the gods and demons, where she is summoned to defeat the formidable demon Raktabija. Raktabija could multiply with every drop of his blood that touched the ground, posing a seemingly insurmountable threat until Kali's intervention – catching each drop of his blood before it hit the ground – thus saving her husband.

In modern times, Kali has become a symbol of feminine empowerment and rebellion against oppression. Her image has been embraced by artists, feminists and countercultural movements worldwide, which appreciate her fierce independence and uncompromising nature.

Kali stands as a powerful embodiment of the divine feminine in Hinduism, challenging devotees to confront the dualities of existence – life and death, creation and destruction.

Given how closely I have witnessed disaster and destruction for the better part of thirty years, I felt like I knew Kali well. I had seen the randomness, the ruthlessness of death so many times. I bore witness to how indiscriminate human suffering often is. I have felt the pain of death's unfairness.

As I kneeled at that temple each time I entered the tunnel, I would think about Kali. I would ask Kali not to kill these men. Not yet anyway. Everyone dies. Everyone's time comes eventually. Death is a debt that must be paid one way or another.

My mission was not to make them immortal. I was not asking Kali to spare them entirely – just for now. This wasn't their time. It wasn't right, it wasn't how they were meant to go.

For the rescuers, I asked her to consider that we were all there to help. We were not doing anything wrong. We were trying to help.

In my head, I was telling her: *Look at me – you're gonna get me real soon. Just not yet, please. I want to do this and go home.*

Not long after I got back to Australia, I was invited to speak at an Indian club in western Melbourne. Hundreds of older Indian people turned out to hear me speak. Or, more accurately, to touch me. They wanted to be near me, having been at the epicentre of what they believe is a religious miracle, in the hope that whatever I possessed might rub off on them.

I took my daughter Hannah with me. A priest handed her a book of religious teachings. She mentioned something about holding onto it for me, assuming it was a gift intended for me. The priest shook his head.

'Arnold doesn't need it,' he smiled. 'He understands.'

Some believe I was chosen by the gods to perform an important role during that rescue. They believe I have been in the presence of gods by discharging my duties as intended. Some have told me that it makes me *god-like*, which is very strange for me to hear. It's quite confronting.

CHAPTER FIFTEEN

SOFT AND SLOW

Human beings have an insatiable appetite for achieving big and challenging goals, one of which is tunnelling through mountains. Mountains are technically complex. Their masses are not meant to be interrupted.

To do it, and to do it well, requires a combination of technical excellence and incredible management skills.

Tunnelling through a mountain is not as simple as getting a really strong drill and defeating this mass of rock. Humans have to do a deal with the mountain. You need to find some kind of harmony. If you take an aggressive or arrogant approach to this act of engineering, you will lose. Every single time.

Every part of an underground project, from the contracts to the procurement, from the resource allocation to selection of the teams, and from the staging and coordination to the reassessment, requires a high level of sophistication to do it well.

You do not get a collapse in a mountain like Silkyara unless a lot of things have gone wrong. They have been going wrong for quite a long time as well. Collapses hold important lessons in how you can better produce underground infrastructure.

It is tempting to think about making a tunnel on the same scale as building a house. Instead of being two storeys high, you want it to be two kilometres long. And instead of it having enough room for a family of five, you want it to have two lanes of traffic for trucks and cars.

It does not work like that. You need a different approach. And intellectually, you need to understand that cheap is not necessarily good.

When you are drilling a hole through a mountain and you do not know what is inside it – and you really don't until you are in it – you have to respect the mountain. You have to engage with it as though it is alive. As tunnellers, we are operating in a different realm, which requires a distinct mindset and approach.

Hello, mountain. I would like to travel through you. I want to do it in a way that is not going to harm you. I do not want to upset you. Can we begin?

Even with all the advanced technology and latest thinking, with every possible scenario anticipated and each risk mitigated, sometimes it just comes down to whether the mountain answers 'yes' or 'no' to that question.

When we got a bigger pipe through the rubble and into the opening where the men were trapped within my first few days onsite, it meant we could stick an endoscope inside.

It was then that the true precariousness of the situation made itself known.

With the vision in hand, I got called into a second meeting room, one I had not been in before. It was totally separate from where everyone usually gathered, and was off-limits to all but the most senior figures involved in the operation. This was where the ministers, military leadership and senior officials hung out for their briefings.

It was in this secret space that candid conversations could be had, without the worry of needing to avoid saying the wrong thing. A negative thing.

A small group of us watched the vision from the endoscope. Then we watched it again. And again. It was chilling. It showed us that, on the side where the men were trapped, the tunnel was essentially being torn apart.

It was like a zipper being opened. Or really, not being opened as intended but ruthlessly ripped apart by force.

Bits of the tunnel's reinforcements were hanging down. A lot of water was dripping from above and weeping from the walls at the side. It looked like the aftermath of a warzone.

From a technical point of view, it was my absolute worst nightmare.

Everything was going wrong. The first auger used to try and dig through the rubble had become stuck and would not budge a millimetre further. A second, more powerful auger was brought to the site.

This new machine was the same type that was used during a massive mine collapse in Chile in 2010, where similarly challenging ground materials had been encountered. There were high hopes of success.

Then, without warning, it blew up.

We had several working theories, giving us backup options should one fall over. Perhaps naively, we did not expect that *all* those ideas would crumble, one by one.

We were carefully drilling in from our end, at the tunnel entrance. We were working on the possibility of drilling down from the top of the mountain, delicately cutting through about eighty-nine metres of rock. And we were toying with the idea of coming in from the other side, through a longer but possibly more stable section of rock stretching 450 metres long.

Many in the management team favoured coming down from the top. It was quick and pretty straightforward. A drilling machine had been deployed to the site, so we could get cracking straight away.

To get the vertical drilling machine up to the top of the mountain, we needed to build a new road through the wild in a hurry. When I say 'road', I am not talking about a beautifully sealed one like you might see in Australia. I mean a relatively flat path gouged through the earth.

A team of roadbuilding women enthusiastically dug the track entirely by hand. They had asked repeatedly to be involved in some way, and given they had experience making similar paths on other road projects – albeit on a much smaller scale – they were brought in. They had the whole job done in just a few days, rockbreaker machines at the front, ladies with shovels following closely behind.

But as they cut through the ground, the women would occasionally slash the roots of trees that had stood there for much, much longer than I have been around. From their wounds, the trees bled small clear streams that glistened in the sun like diamonds. It was like they were crying.

The mountain was upset. We were ripping away its vegetation, piercing its skin and tearing at its very fabric. I felt the mountain was crying in pain and in sorrow from its lacerated tree roots.

Whenever I saw some of these tree tears, I would carefully climb up and wipe them away with my finger. It was my unusual way of apologising, I guess. I was trying to make peace with what we were doing to the mountain.

The whole process caused me enormous sadness. I had spent some time up there on the mountaintop and had grown fond of it. It was quiet, serene and beautiful. It pained me to think of an enormous machine being dragged right through the middle of it.

But it was necessary. It was a viable option and we had to explore it, for the sake of those forty-one men.

With the help of a colleague, I surveyed the area and found the perfect spot. It was the ideal location to set up a drilling rig and begin tearing through the ground and rock, in hopes of reaching the trapped workers almost 100 metres below. I felt confident. From this location, we could pierce the crown of the tunnel above that small cavern.

But it sat in the middle of a beautiful little valley. The point where we had to work was the exact spot I did not want to disturb. An ancient stream was running through the forest nearby, its gentle trickles audible from where we were standing. In the distance appeared to be the remnants of ancient rock fences and road markings, harking back to a settlement from long in the past.

We were even relatively close to villages. While wandering around, we regularly met figures who suddenly popped out of the trees while on their way to wherever they were going. They lived a kilometre or two further up the hill in simple but homely settlements. No electricity, no running water, but everything they needed to create communities.

I went back to the site to tell the rescue leaders that I had found the ideal spot. It was not a little bit to the left or just a smidge to the right. It was bang on.

'It is as though the gods themselves put this piece of rock there, because that location is absolutely perfect,' I said with a tinge of sadness.

It did not feel perfect. It felt like an invasion. I wondered if the mountain felt the same way, because it just kept moving.

If you have never been inside a tunnel while it is under construction, it can be hard to picture what it looks like.

Think of an inverted wine barrel where the steel hoops that surround the staves of wood are on the inside instead. That was what we were dealing with. A half-sphere cut into rock with bits of lattice and steel that were meant to keep the mountain above in place.

Each day brought fresh ground shifts, which, at best, sent small rocks falling from the top of the tunnel. At worst, chilling loud cracking sounds bounced wildly off the walls, causing us all to drop what we were doing and run. Hardhats are no match for massive rocks. You die.

Advanced and sensitive measurement tools were giving us second-by-second data, which showed the mountain was continuously moving. Sometimes, it was subtle and relatively gentle, as far as potential collapses go. Other times, the readings were enough to send a prolonged shiver down my spine.

We were faced with the constant risk that we could trigger a major landslide or catastrophic collapse. And there was a lot going on.

We had the augering team, which had been trying to get through from the beginning. They had consistently run into difficulties. Augering over that distance is not overly common. Adding to the complexities was the amount of steel, machines and concrete mixed in among the rock.

We also had the team working on the vertical shaft from the top of the mountain, trying to dig a space big enough for a rescue capsule to fit into.

Another smaller shaft, also coming from above, was being dug as a kind of exploratory tunnel. As well as giving us more insight into what was going on, we figured it could act as a backup to the tube sending food, air and medicine to the trapped men, in case we had another collapse down in the tunnel.

A team was working on the other side of the collapse, but the more the earth shifted, the clearer it became that the whole thing was unstable.

We all became quite risk-averse over time. The more I pondered it, the less comfortable I felt with the approach the rest of the team had the most faith in. Coming in from above.

I had seen just how powdery and brittle the rock above us was on my first day. I was also concerned about the possibility of concealed pockets of water within the rock. We could not be sure, not 100 per cent certain, if or where they were. If we happened to pierce one, it could inundate the tunnel below, condemning the trapped men to a torturous death by drowning.

I had recently come across some shocking vision of that exact type of disaster in a tunnel project about 100 kilometres away. A hidden water body was pierced during construction works and almost instantly inundated the whole thing.

In the video, you can see uncontrollable torrents of water rushing furiously out of several entrances. There's almost no prospect of surviving such an event should you happen to be inside at the time.

We could not risk that happening here. The trapped men would perish. Those of us on the other side who weren't crushed to death against rock and machinery from a wall of force would perish, too.

When the vertical shaft was complete, one of the ideas was to dangle a man upside down on a rope almost 100 metres long with an oxyacetylene torch to cut through the final obstacle, a steel girder we would encounter in the crown.

The more I heard it, the uneasier I grew. We could not do this. We had to stop.

'Guys, the goal is forty-one men home safe and no-one else hurt. Right?'

There was nodding around the table.

'Now, who's here from the emergency services?'

A chap raised his hand.

'OK, so how likely is it we're going to be able to dangle a man upside down on a hundred-metre-long rope while he's holding a piece of machinery and not hurt him?'

It seemed I had a point. It was back to the drawing board.

On our side of the tunnel, we were using drones to conduct surveying and mapping of the situation. The drones produced a digital drawing that provided a colour-coded overview of the stability of the rock.

Red and pink means run away. There was a lot of red and pink.

The drone data showed us that the tunnel was collapsing on our side. Every single day. The initial collapse was still ongoing. It had never stopped – it had just slowed down.

We also discovered that in the mountain above where the collapse occurred was an enormous, forty-metre-high hollow space. Just picture how unstable and dangerous that scenario is. That is a lot of unsupported rock just waiting to come down.

Down below, inside the tunnel, both sides of the rubble were extremely unstable. It was a disastrous position to be in because one wrong move could mean we'd all be killed. Everyone knew it, too. Not a single person involved in that rescue was oblivious to what was at stake.

On top of the mapping data from the drones, the endoscopic view showed us that the crown of the tunnel – the inside top of it – was also close to caving in. If we banged into it from above with our cutting machine, there was a strong possibility of disaster.

Some important Italian friends of mine let us use their satellite to map movements on the surface, too. We were checking – from space – if the entire mountain was about to blow. The satellite data showed that the surface was still stable, which gave me hope. My Indian colleagues were somewhat baffled that I had mates in such high places.

The more the hours and days stretched on, the more I felt we had to calm down and slow down. Quick could be very risky. If we rushed things, which I firmly believed we did not have to, given the men were alive, then it might all be over in an instant.

Having said that, I was hugely conscious of the need to not undermine any of the management team or other experts. I could not just barrel in and run over the top of everyone, furiously shooting down their suggestions and screeching to get my point across.

I had to remain cool, calm and hopeful. I had to gently steer the thinking towards a more considered approach. But the approach would be painfully slow. I could feel patience wearing thin.

'What if we consider this . . .' I would offer, when

Eight years after first meeting each other and thanks to my matchmaking daughter Hannah and an Excel spreadsheet, Divina and I got married in 2023.

In September 2023, just weeks before the Silkyara tunnel collapse, I visited some of the most extreme tunnels in the world to investigate tunnel instability. This is in Mponeng gold mine in South Africa, which is the deepest mine in the world.

A Russian helicopter as old as myself was waiting for me at Dehradun Airport to take me to the tunnel on 19 November – a week after the collapse.

One of the first things I did after getting off the helicopter was to pay my respects to the Hindu goddess Kali at the little temple that had been rebuilt at the entrance to the tunnel. But I should have taken off my shoes before kneeling.

I hadn't planned on going to the Himalayas so I didn't have any warm clothes with me. I was given a camouflage snow suit – standard gear for military operations in the snow. My fellow rescue workers thought I looked cool!

Early on in the rescue a number of ministers showed up to inspect the scene. One was Sunita Vidyarthi, who wasn't wearing a helmet, so I gave her mine. After that we became friends, and I was trusted.

In the final days of the rescue, a senior commander invited me for a cup of tea and biscuits on top of the mountain, to discuss how the operation was going. It was a bizarre occasion, with the linen tablecloth and English Breakfast tea!

Maintaining friendships with the rescue team was so important. These people would soon risk their lives by crawling through a small pipe to rescue the trapped men.

Ouch! I accidentally packed my daughter's work boots instead of my own and developed painful blisters. But it reminded me with every step that I was saving other people's children's lives.

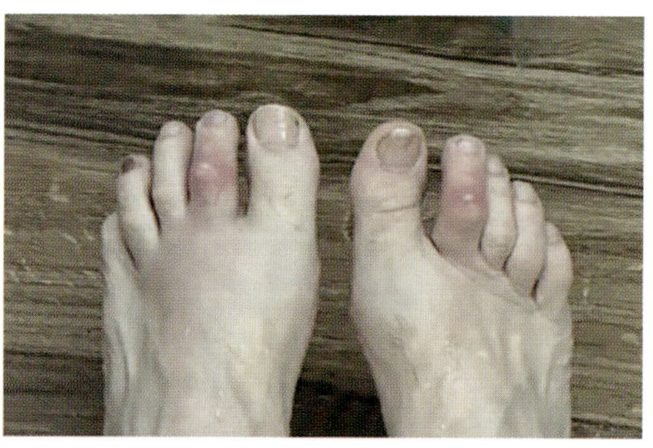

During the Covid lockdowns, Col from Warburton taught me how to weld. Here I am in the welding pit at the tunnel with soldiers and tunnel fabricators designing and building rescue equipment out of whatever scraps we could find.

On 27 November I swapped my white hardhat, which signified that I was a manager, with a yellow hardhat, indicating I was a worker. This lifted morale at a time when the team was becoming depressed, as nothing was working. We were now all on the same team.

At a briefing with the rescue team the day before we got the workers out. I told them if there was another collapse during the rescue that we would get them out. They knew we had their backs.

Vertical drilling on top of the mountain is paused to mitigate collapse and flooding risk.

Below left: On 29 November after the rescue, National Disaster Response Force personnel and I went to the temple on top of the mountain and thanked local deity Baba Boukhnag.

Above: By chance on 30 November, after everyone was freed, I met twenty-one of the rescued men at Dehradun Airport. We were scheduled on the same flight.

When I got home the Sri Vakrathunda Vinayagar temple in Melbourne welcomed Divina, Trisha and myself as if we were Hindu and family.

After the rescue, children throughout India dressed up as me for superhero fancy dress days at school. This is Sai Sajnyaa Manosundar from Aditya Vidyashram Primary School in Puducherry. I promised her I would go and visit her school.

Harrison Edwards

Maggie, Yvonne and Becky from the local church in Monbulk painted welcome home signs for my homecoming.

Harrison Edwards

Monbulk welcomes me home on 5 December 2023.

My sister Helena and mother Norma with a pre-rescue portrait from Ken (jeweller and resident artist at Monbulk Jewellers). Ken wanted to paint me with my pet emu before I was a public figure, for the 2023 Archibald Prize.

Murali Surya, realism artist, Hindu philosopher and particle physics engineer, believed it was his destiny to paint me. For hundreds of hours we shared secrets in his studio. I was 'too white' to be painted in the nude – luckily! It was entered in the 2024 Archibald Prize, but didn't make the final cut.

Here I am playing Santa at the Monbulk Produce Market – and I don't need a fake beard! I'm the original good Santa and love it!

discussions began to stray away from the slow-and-gentle approach I was trying to get us all to accept.

'Let's just remember that . . .' I would reiterate, if the temptation to rush cropped up once more.

I focused on the positives. On the safest options in front of us. On the need for us to unite and remain optimistic.

Optimism would help prevent us from making mistakes. It would keep us grounded and steely eyed on the objective – getting these men out alive and not killing ourselves in the process.

The vertical drilling team got to within a few metres of the section where the men were trapped. They were within shouting distance. When the roaring drilling machine was switched off, the two groups separated by rock could hear the faint murmurs of each other.

Even though we were so close, we had a meeting and decided the risk was too great. As difficult as it was to do, we abandoned the idea.

But the fact of the matter was that we were worried we would trigger an avalanche or release one of those concealed water bodies, killing everyone. There was no other choice.

The amount of self-control required to stop and wait, especially knowing we were so close to the men, was incredible. Talk about resisting temptation. I cannot remember ever encountering a lure quite as strong as the one we reluctantly walked away from that day.

It was hugely admirable. It showed that everyone was part of a big team, working together and doing so selflessly. No ego. No self-interest. We were all on the same page.

We showed restraint, grace and calmness. We cooperated and collaborated. We heard and respected each other's views. And we proceeded together, as one.

I repeated it regularly to the group – a new kind of mantra. If we have a choice between hard and soft, go soft. If we have a choice between fast and slow, go slow. It became a shared philosophy among us all.

This simple but important phrase helped to keep us all grounded. It kept us on track. It reminded us of not just the enormous risk, but what was at stake.

The only way we stood a chance was if we approached the rescue in a soft way. In a sense, we had to trick the mountain. We had to carefully burrow our way into where the men were trapped. If we just smashed our way in with big machines, the mountain would have felt us and the whole thing would have collapsed.

No-one was dead. No-one had been hurt. The men were getting food, water, medicine and oxygen. Maintaining the status quo was an admirable achievement. It meant we didn't have to rush or take unnecessary risks, we could be clear, calm and calculated in our approach.

It meant the men who were trapped were safe, but so were we. If you rush, you don't just risk those you are trying to rescue, but also yourselves on the other side of the fallen rock.

For as long as I can remember, I have had a strong ability to bring people together. Not in a kumbaya sense. There is no campfire guitar singalong involved in my approach to connecting people.

Gail calls me a chameleon. I can adapt to different surroundings and put people at ease by not seeming too much like an outsider. Whether it is a worksite, a meeting full of people from different cultural backgrounds, a stuffy courtroom where formalities and pageantry loom large, a rural farm or a soiree at an ambassador's mansion, I rarely feel out of place. I can blend in.

When you blend in, when you are non-threatening and do not seem out of place, people let their guards down.

I seem to be able to bridge the gap between pretty rigid specialities – science and law, engineering and human rights. Usually, engineers tend to hate lawyers. Lawyers are not fond of engineers either. Not many people like the scientists. And the human rights guys probably hate everyone.

To bring all these people together and unite them in the same room is no small feat. Usually, in meetings like these, everyone is armed with their own heavy stack of binders and folders. They are there to present their case, usually quite sternly, and do not care much about what anyone else has to say.

Somehow, I am able to not just get them into a room, but get them all on the same page. I can unite groups to stand as one and subscribe to a shared vision.

I think it is a simple case of seeing everyone as human. We might wear different clothes, speak different languages and have different priorities, but we are all the same.

Like I explained, I was never given a defined role when I arrived at the tunnel site. I was simply asked to help. As the days wore on and nerves became frayed, my purpose became crystal clear.

The sense of urgency was growing as each new day arrived. Pressure was building and I worried that the temptation to rush, for the sake of making any kind of progress, would become irresistible.

It felt like nothing we tried was working. Everything had gone wrong so far. We heard that some of the trapped workers had developed gastro and were unwell.

Things were going downhill. The mood was very flat.

Somehow, I had to give everyone a sense of hope. I had to focus everyone's minds on a future where everyone gets out and no-one gets hurt.

My role was to calm everyone down, remind those sitting around the table that the men were still safe – we were getting them food, water and medicines – and that we could go slow and soft.

This wasn't just a job. It wasn't a set of challenges that I could examine, strategise and solve from a distance. I wasn't simply contributing to a task.

I was immersed in it. It became a part of me.

I was on the mountain. I was in the mountain. I was with the people – the rescuers, executives, spiritual gurus, locals and the press. I was part of that eclectic cohort, rather than a distant observer of it.

And even though I could not see them, and we were separated by a huge and volatile pile of rock and construction rubbish, I felt like I was with those men. Some kind of invisible connection between us penetrated the impenetrable.

I was consumed by all of it.

If this whole thing was a horror film, it would be as though a poltergeist had possessed me.

Maybe I do need an exorcism of some kind after all that has happened. It does feel like this experience is still with me all this time later. Although I would probably be a little concerned about what was left inside my head after that nightmarish demon had been banished.

At least it has plenty of company.

CHAPTER SIXTEEN

IN THE SPOTLIGHT, AND THE FIRING LINE

To this day, I cannot quite figure out how so many members of the Indian and international press got up to the tunnel rescue site so quickly. By the time I got there, more than 100 journalists, representing a whole host of print, television and online outlets, had set up camp.

Even the BBC had a reporter up there, who filed daily stories with the latest updates, which were then beamed around the world.

This was a delicate operation with a number of moving parts and lots of people involved. Among those playing a role were several members of the Indian Defence Force. Despite that, the media was largely free to move around as they pleased.

They were not allowed into the tunnel without permission and an escort, of course, but aside from that, most had a tendency to just . . . roam. I would turn a corner or venture out from a demountable room and there one – or several – would be.

Some in the press pack never quite knew what to make of me. If they formed a picture in their mind of an international expert, someone who led a massive global body and had a lot of experience in complex operations, I highly doubt they saw my face. And they definitely did not imagine my personality.

I was asked once to identify the biggest challenge facing us. I responded, 'The mountain.'

In another exchange, I was asked to explain what I had meant when I described myself as 'old-school' in an off-hand remark. I showed off my compass, which I carry in my pocket.

'How's this for old-school?' I beamed.

They still did not understand the point I was trying to make.

Those reporters were expecting a serious engineer, who rattled off numbers and equations and technical processes, as though speaking an alien language. I spoke clearly in a way that everyone could understand. They thought this foreign expert was going to be gruff, rigid and sterile. I was anything but.

I was myself. I was Arnold – the one you get anywhere you encounter me. That style was quite disarming. I was calm, clear and even a bit jovial. There seemed to be no reason for that other than my belief that we were going to get these men out, and it proved to be infectious.

Until it was not.

On Day Eleven of the rescue mission, I was asked to appear on one of India's biggest news programs. The previous day, I began to sense a subtle shift in mood, both on the site and among the journalists. Patience was wearing thin. When the interview request came in, the media's frustration and the dipping mood among rescue workers were enough of a motivation for me to agree, with a sole mission in my mind.

I had to lift people's spirits. The frustrated journalists, who had been watching on from a distance for more than a week. The exhausted rescue workers, who were terrified we might fail. The hundreds of millions of Indians watching on nervously, glued to television sets and phone screens, who were praying for a miracle.

We were dealing with the most extreme conditions. The mountain was extremely volatile and a single misstep could bring the whole thing down around us.

Despite that, and in spite of knowing what I knew, I assured the anchor and those watching that we would have terrific news very soon. I focused on the positives of the mission. We had a pipe in to get the men everything they needed to stay healthy and alive. We had a team of local and international experts, who were collaborating in a way I had never witnessed before in my career. No-one was dead and that was a very good – and rare – state to be in.

As much as the press pack seemed to like me, I was not immune from being taken to task. The longer things drew on, the more antsy the media became.

In the later days of the rescue operation, the journalists began to turn on me. I understand it. There was a great deal of frustration that things were taking longer than anyone had hoped. Even though we were well away from my self-imposed deadline of Christmas, there was a sense from the outside looking in that we weren't making enough progress.

Or, at least, progress that could be seen by those outside the tunnel itself. Perhaps more accurately, progress that could be reported around the clock without seeming repetitive to viewers.

By that point, we were less than ten metres away from the men. No doubt, it seemed like a really short distance to those watching at home. What was taking us so long? Just get on with it!

But those ten metres might as well have been a thousand kilometres.

On 25 November – after about fourteen days of rescue efforts – the auger catastrophically failed. It could not be repaired. I had to announce that we had stopped drilling after the auger exploded when we hit steel. It was like I had walked into a lion's den holding a deer carcass. The journalists pounced immediately – the lions were starving.

I was surrounded by a dozen or more reporters with their microphones jammed in my face, with several cameras trained on me.

'When are they coming home?' one screamed.

'When? When, Arnold? When?' another shouted.

Tensions were running high. The press pack was exhausted, sweaty from standing beneath a blaring sun for days on end and desperate for answers.

I tried to repeat my mantra of hope, that these forty-one men would be home by Christmas, but it was struggling to ring true at that moment.

'That's a long time, Arnold,' a journalist sighed.

I tried to explain that if we rushed, if we panicked because one of our approaches had not worked and we felt like we needed to do something else quickly, just for the sake of looking like we were making progress, then it could spell disaster. We could cause an even bigger problem in the tunnel. In an instant, we could hurtle ourselves back to square one. And that was best-case. At worst, we could kill those forty-one men. And probably ourselves.

But they could smell blood. And without disrespecting any friends in the media, journalists are sharks. That is their job. They need to hunt for stories and, more and more these days, they need to make them compelling enough to draw in a smaller and smaller collection of eyeballs.

Snippets from that heated press conference were edited together by one major media outlet into a package that set the scene for failure. Watching it back in hindsight, I can see that those observing were starting to wonder if there really was going to be a happy ending. It was evident they were starting to get ready for the horrible reality that we might fail and everyone would die.

The news package that aired was set to a gloomy soundtrack of ominous music that would be right at home in a horror film. The graphics were black and white. The B-roll vision from the rescue site had a darkened filter applied to it.

Reading between the lines, the message was clear: *We have lost faith in you, and when this goes wrong, it will be all your fault.*

No pressure.

CHAPTER SEVENTEEN

MY MATE PUFFING BILLY

Some of the most significant work I have done has seen me not earn a single red cent. This work has meant a great deal to many people, in bleak situations and not-so-life-and-death ones, from an historic railway to a series of catastrophic fires that took a staggering number of lives.

But each was important on its own terms, and I was happy and keen to help. And to do so for free.

If you are from Victoria, or have spent some time here, chances are you will be familiar with one of our most beloved icons, Puffing Billy.

The Puffing Billy Railway runs through the southern foothills of the Dandenong Ranges, not too far from where I live. The line is one of several that opened in the early 1900s, starting at Belgrave and continuing to Lakeside Station and Gembrook. Its original purpose was to service farmers and timber manufacturers in the region. It ceased formal operations in 1955.

When its commercial service ended, a small but loyal group of locals formed the Puffing Billy Preservation Society. They wanted to see the railway run forever and worked tirelessly to restore sections of the track, keeping the love for Billy going strong throughout the mid- to late 1900s.

These days, the Puffing Billy Railway runs each day, taking tourists – and a whole lot of kids – for rides on a collection of beautiful steam engines. The infrastructure has been lovingly restored and reflects the bygone early of the early 1900s. About half a million visitors come to see Billy each year.

Part of the charm and fascination of Puffing Billy is the carriage fleet. The carriages are open-sided cars built to a mostly original design and are well-suited to tourist traffic. They offer visitors the chance to go for a ride with their legs dangling off the edge. That special opportunity is part of what made Puffing Billy so famous and beloved.

Professionally, I am fairly highly regarded in the railway safety sector, and have been active in this space for decades. I have dealt with issues relating to train travel underground, which is arguably one of the most dangerous environments you can put a railway in.

Puffing Billy is not a theme park. It is still under the control of regulatory authorities, so it needs to be deemed 100 per cent safe. The difficulty for the authorities is that they are used to dealing with modern infrastructure, not historic railways from a time when things were done a little differently.

There has long been a complicated tension between the bureaucrats and the custodians of Puffing Billy. At various points, the black-and-white view has been that, because the operation does not run like a modern railway, it must be unsafe.

It has no doors that lock everybody into a carriage, like you find on modern trains. It has no long-line radio facilities, where announcements can be made to passengers. It's a steam train. It's a very different animal.

Reports began to emerge about some unruly behaviour among visitors. People hanging off the back, running up and down, skylarking – that kind of thing. I was asked to audit the service and make some recommendations about how they could ensure passenger safety.

I was actively involved in that process when a bus slammed into the side of a train in March 2018. The vehicle had failed to stop at a level crossing. Miraculously, no-one was killed. But it was a wake-up call. Suddenly, the regulator was very concerned. It was like: 'What are we doing here? This isn't right.'

I suggested that operators should get in front of a looming headache by immediately stopping people hanging their legs off the side of the carriages. Somehow, the accident had not seen anyone lose their legs, but it could have happened – and it could again in the future.

This was devastating for those who knew and loved Puffing Billy for that very reason – being able to dangle from the side of it. It was a thrilling and fun experience, especially for young people.

But we put an end to it, just for the time being, while we came up with a solution that could keep Puffing Billy going without posing a serious risk.

The solution was a re-engineered seat design that could shift people's centre of gravity by tilting it backwards a bit. The idea was that by moving how the body was positioned when dangling over the edge, we could significantly reduce the risk of injury or death in the event of a catastrophe.

I lived in the neighbourhood, so Puffing Billy was special to me, just as it was to everyone in the area who knew it well. I could not watch on as its future hung in the balance. I got to work doing what I do in every scenario when something has gone wrong. I analysed the problem and worked on finding a solution with the team.

The seat design made riding Puffing Billy a safe pleasure, ensuring its continued survival. This longevity means future generations will be able to experience it, just as countless have before them.

After four years and plenty of back and forth with authorities, Puffing Billy was back operating with its famed window seats. Together with other experts, also offering their skills and time for free, I helped to save a cherished icon.

On 3 July 2009, a fire broke out in a high-rise residential building in Camberwell in London's south. The tragedy would have major ramifications and offer a variety of lessons – most of which, horrifyingly, were seemingly ignored.

Lakanal House was a fourteen-storey social housing complex, comprising ninety-eight flats. Each was a two-level maisonette, with two bedrooms and a bathroom in front when you entered the front door, and a staircase leading up to a kitchen and lounge room.

Each unit had an emergency exit from the upper-level lounge and kitchen to a balcony. The largest of the two bedrooms also had a fire exit into the corridor.

A faulty television set in a unit on the twelfth floor sparked a fire on the afternoon of 3 July. As the ferocious blaze spread quickly through the building, the fire system had been so poorly maintained that escaping was rendered virtually impossible.

The central stairwell was almost instantly filled with thick, choking and blinding smoke. Residents were trapped inside their flats. Some tried to escape through the windows. You could hear panicked screams and pleas for help from blocks away.

Fire crews were on the scene within minutes, but getting the fire under control was no small feat. The building's design and the scale of the blaze presented major challenges for them. As a result, six people died, including three children. Dozens more were injured, several seriously.

When I'm not famous in tunnelling, I am pretty highly regarded in fire safety. After the Lakanal House fire, it seemed clear that the authorities wanted to blame the tragedy on the fire brigade's response.

They needed a culprit that an angry public could unite in condemning. The firefighters who put their own lives on the line to save innocent people were offered up like lambs to the slaughter.

With disasters like this, you tend to find that those who are really to blame get off scot-free. When the going gets tough, they are nowhere to be seen. Instead, they find a scapegoat so they never bear any responsibility for the tragedy.

That is what happened here. The faceless, nameless people involved in years and years of ham-fisted refurbishments, shonky or non-existent maintenance of life-saving safety systems, and a general lack of care for society's most vulnerable who called that death trap of a building home, suffered no consequences.

Conveniently, it tends to be really hard, if not impossible, to pin the blame on those who deserve it.

Social housing in the United Kingdom (UK) had become a nightmare. The government was effectively broke and severe austerity measures saw vital funds slashed. The social housing program was gutted, and quality and safety standards suffered as a result.

I was called in the days after the fire, and asked if I could come to London to look at what had happened and offer an independent opinion of the root cause of the tragedy. My findings would help with a coronial inquiry that was due to take place.

I sought special leave from the Courts of England and Wales to be able to appear in my capacity as a barrister. That sort of thing happens from time to time, when someone registered in a different jurisdiction has cause to come before the courts. I jumped through all the required hoops, getting character references from Australia, then fronted up to have it approved.

Before that, I conducted my investigation. I discovered just how professionally corrupt the situation was. The popular narrative that the fire brigade was to blame for the loss of life was totally wrong. They never, ever stood a chance – and neither did those people living inside Lakanal House.

I visited an identical social housing complex, Madame Curie House, which was a sister building to Lakanal and had many of the same issues. The only difference was that it had not yet gone up in flames. But I found out that it very well could, imminently, unless major changes were made.

These buildings were in a rough part of London. I was warned not to venture out there at night because I had a high chance of being robbed, bashed or both. And I could die. Because of this type of danger, many of the social housing flats had bars on the doors and windows, so those inside could feel a greater sense of safety.

There were makeshift barriers on fire stairs to prevent those who should not be there from gaining access. But this meant residents' emergency exit access was also prevented. On top of that, barriers to stop smoke and flames from getting between different areas and passing between floors did not work as they should.

In one case, I went up to a fire door and pushed it with my finger. It was not like I shoved it with my big, boofy hand. I just gently pushed on it, and the whole thing collapsed. What a nightmare.

During renovations, like in Lakanal House, spaces between floors that should have been sealed – to protect residents if there was a fire – were missing.

The report I wrote was scathing but I thought it would still be well-received. Here I was, an expert in the field, offering a timely warning about the same kind of issues in a nearby building. I expressed my concern and made several recommendations about how Madame Curie House could be made safe. I made clear that recent renovations and repairs were simply not up to standard. I do not know where the renovation money went, I have no idea what workmen busied themselves with during the project, because the whole thing was a shit show.

I thought the people in charge needed to know. I had a responsibility – a duty – to tell anyone who would listen.

It was not taken well.

When word got out that I had written this report, I was accused of being some kind of fraudster. An ambulance chaser looking to capitalise on the tragedy for my own personal gain. My motives were questioned and I was subjected to a minor character assassination.

I had pissed off some important people by pointing out just how thoroughly they were failing countless people in their care.

A senior barrister who was working on the coronial inquiry phoned me. He thought the report was fantastic but he was not surprised I was meeting such a fierce string of attacks. I was some random who had come out of left field, attacking the status quo and embarrassing those who were close to, if not right in the centre of, responsibility.

When I got to court, I stood and made my application for leave to appear. It should have just been a formality, which the court agreed with and approved. I had everything I needed. This kind of thing had been done before many, many times. But the judge was not having it.

We went back and forth a number of times. I explained my case, and she would rule against me. I would offer a rebuttal and a new argument, and she would find against me. I was floored. And devastated.

I had come all the way to the UK. I had done all this really good and important work. I had put a huge amount of effort into being able to appear on behalf of the fire brigade to make clear that they were being wrongly blamed.

The barrister who had phoned me about my report called again. He could see how unfair the ruling was and asked if I might be interested in offering my expert advice for his case. I agreed and we worked together for the next several weeks. I helped to convey the major engineering issues within Lakanal House.

That satisfied me. Sure, I was not appearing as counsel, but I was helping to make a difference. I played a role in making the UK a bit safer for people who live in social housing. I had helped to expose the serious shortcomings, informing the findings of the coronial inquiry and its important recommendations.

The inquiry found that several catastrophic failures in the building's fire safety management system contributed to the severity of the blaze. The local council and social housing management authorities came under scrutiny for knowing about some of these major risks and failing to address them.

The Lakanal House tragedy exposed the serious issues plaguing safety and quality standards in social housing blocks in the UK. An excellent original design, entirely compromised by haphazard and shockingly dangerous additions over the years, meant countless people were at serious risk should a similar tragedy occur.

I felt like I had done something good. I went home and did not really think about it again, until eight years later when almost the exact same thing happened again. Only this time, many more people died and the level of public fury was explosive.

On 14 June 2017, the world watched with horror as live television coverage showed Grenfell Tower in the London suburb of North Kensington engulfed in flames.

The twenty-four storey Grenfell Tower was home to several hundred people occupying a mix of one- and two-bedroom units, of which there were 129 in total.

At about one o'clock in the morning, a short-circuiting refrigerator on the fourth floor sparked a fire. Within moments, flames began lapping the outside of the block, thanks to the highly combustible exterior cladding, which had only recently been installed during a renovation and refurbishment of the social housing flats.

No-one stood a chance. The blaze spread so quickly through the building that much of it was engulfed about fifteen minutes after emergency services were alerted. It took 250 firefighters, working from seventy fire engines, some sixty hours to completely extinguish it.

The flames stretched to every single floor within thirty minutes.

Seventy-two people perished – a horrifying loss of life. Several children were among the dead, with the youngest being a six-month-old girl. A pregnant woman who survived later lost her baby during childbirth.

In Grenfell's original design, thick walls and special fire doors should prevent the spread of fire if one was to break out. As a result, the building – like many other similar structures – was the subject of a so-called 'stay put' order. In a blaze, authorities would order those inside to shelter in place until told otherwise.

Like with Lakanal House, Grenfell's fire-safety system was severely lacking. It had a single central staircase from which to escape. There was no central fire alarm. A number of renovations in the almost five decades since its construction saw many of the original fire safety features altered or entirely removed.

For years, these and other concerns had been documented but ignored by authorities. The public was rightly infuriated. Multiple investigations and a public inquiry were launched, which exposed a troubling mix of regulatory failures, poor building practices and inadequate safety measures.

Hang on a minute, I thought. *How can this have happened?*

I got on a plane straight away and went to London.

I did not have a real role, but immersed myself in the local community at Grenfell and spoke to anyone who would talk to me. Initially, I faced some suspicion. I was clearly an outsider. The worry among locals was that I was a spy of some sort, sent by the government to find out what people were up to. Such was the level of anger and upset at what had happened that no-one really trusted anyone.

I was sure that it could not be a case of those inquiry recommendations being ignored. I was certain that something else catastrophic must have gone on, and that this was not a preventable tragedy.

But it was. The more I spoke to people, the clearer it became that, once again, a corrupt system had seen money meant to improve these buildings and ensure people's safety go God knows where. Into people's pockets, I suspect.

I started interviewing people about what had actually happened in Grenfell. Like with Lakanal House, the authorities were looking for someone to blame. Again, they circled around the fire brigade. They argued that the instruction from the emergency services to residents to shelter in place was incorrect, but that was not the case at all.

Had Grenfell been properly maintained, had the myriad safety issues that were well known and clearly documented been addressed, the policy to stay in place would have worked.

How could the fire brigade have known that the building was such a mess? How could they have anticipated that the issues were so severe that the policy was doomed to fail? It was a systematic institutional failure in the delivery of safe homes for vulnerable people.

When you go to the police, you expect that specially trained officers will assist you. When you go to the dentist, you expect that the professional, who is abundantly qualified and best-placed to treat you, will get it right. Why should the provision of housing be any different?

Those in charge of social housing in the UK had a pretty simple job. They had all the information at their disposal to make sure the buildings they housed people in were safe, at the very least. They did virtually nothing to prevent Grenfell becoming not just unsafe, but a death trap.

I teamed up with a forensic arson investigator and we spent weeks investigating what had happened. Alongside other experts, we concluded that the facade of the building, which had recently been installed in a refurbishment, was to blame. But that was only half the truth.

Even with that same flammable cladding, had the fire engineering of Grenfell been up to scratch – had the safety systems worked as intended, had they not been bastardised by morons working on the cheap, or compromised and never audited – people inside would have been fine.

It still would have looked like an explosive Roman candle, but residents would have been safe in their homes because the compartmentation fire systems would have worked, and worked really well.

Instead, fire doors were propped open or removed. Walls had been busted through without any fire protection being retained. Barriers between floors were non-existent. Emergency exit doors had been welded shut.

I was furious. I could not believe that the exact same thing had been allowed to happen again. I was incensed that good people trying their best to protect the residents had been blamed for something that was not their fault.

I was sickened that those who bore the true responsibility for this shocking loss of life were going to be let off the hook again.

So, using my own money and calling on technical experts and computer engineers I knew, I built a web application called Tower Inspector. It allowed anyone who lived in a social housing tower to self-diagnose its fire-engineering capability.

They could upload photos, put in various bits of information, and fire-safety specialists would carefully assess it at the other end. The building residents would then be empowered with the knowledge of precisely what was wrong. And so could the media.

I had a brilliant journalist from the BBC's radio division follow me around and watch what I was doing. His subsequent reporting put a great deal of pressure on the authorities to front up and answer some serious questions about what the fuck was going on in the system.

I felt stupid that I had trusted the authorities to do the right thing after the Lakanal House tragedy. I felt foolish that I had put faith in the system to work as it should and for innocent people to be protected.

So this time around, I bypassed all that nonsense and tried to make real change myself. Tower Inspector did some good in exposing many, many problems in buildings right across the UK.

But ultimately, the app was a bit of a flop. I learned the hard way that professional services, like fire engineering, cannot be delegated to non-professionals. Or if it can be, I never figured it out. I failed, but I tried.

The anger stemming from the Grenfell disaster was such that authorities, those in charge who had received the Lakanal House report and hidden it in a drawer, could not ignore the will of the people.

I am constantly bothered by how some people seem to be so apathetic about other people's hardship. It goes beyond not caring – in some cases, it is downright nasty.

Last year, I was in Washington, DC for work. I was at the airport getting ready to fly out when this guy approached me. It was weird. We were inside the terminal and he was dressed like a construction worker.

He asked me if I had any spare money. I handed over whatever was left in my wallet in US dollars. He smiled, took it and walked off. About five minutes later, I felt a tap on my shoulder and turned around. There he was again.

'I just want to talk to you,' he said, almost in a whisper. 'I've been here all morning, working, collecting luggage trolleys in the car park to take back to the luggage carousel. I lost my job recently as a construction worker and I couldn't stand doing nothing. You giving me that money made me feel seen. Now I can go and have some lunch.'

It meant so little to me. But it meant a lot to him.

I didn't consider his intentions. I didn't ask him what he needed the money for. I didn't interrogate him on why he was begging in such an unexpected place. I trusted that he knew what was right – the rest of it was none of my business.

I trusted myself in knowing that helping him in a small way was the right thing to do.

What difference does it make to my life to be kind? Nothing.

I once gave money to a beggar on the street in Melbourne. The person I was walking with scoffed, telling me I had probably just been scammed. That immediate dismissal of a perfect stranger doesn't sit well with me. Even considering that possibility gets in the way of the intention of my act – to show someone a little kindness and some mercy.

Who cares if they spend that money on alcohol? Who cares if they don't really need it as much as they have implied?

When we do not take each other at face value, when we discard people because they do not act or look like we think they should, we do a disservice to each other as human beings.

'Jeez, what did you invoice for that?' I was asked recently at a barbeque, when talking about what was involved with the India rescue.

It had not occurred to me that most people probably assumed I had charged for my services. Because of the enormous complexities, because of the lengthy journey to get there, and because of the unbelievable, miraculous outcome, I must have benefited handsomely in a compensation sense, right?

Absolutely not.

The truth is that I did not make one cent from this job, nor did I expect to. The idea of charging for my role in the rescue never crossed my mind. It was never a commercial opportunity, but a contribution to the community – to the tunnelling community, to the men and women who risk their lives working underground, to humanity, I suppose.

A friend in need called me. Innocent people needed help. I was in a position to contribute. So that is what I did. It is really as simple as that.

It wasn't just me. Several other volunteers also offered their expertise, tools and manpower for free. Like me, they believed intrinsically that it was called for. We needed to help. It was our duty.

One of them was a fellow Australian, Chris Cooper. Chris commanded a team working on one of the backup plans, an emergency horizontal entry dug with a tunnel-boring machine from the side of the mountain. He was seconded from another tunnel project in the Himalayas, where he dropped everything to lend a hand.

In just a matter of days, he designed and constructed an entire tunnel boring machine (TBM) launch site. He brilliantly led a top-notch team of workers to give everyone not just another option, but greater hope. And did I mention his samosas? Chris would share his home-cooked food with us too – kindness from the kitchen has universal appeal.

No single person saved those forty-one men. Chris, me, so many people played critical roles. The rescue required every single piece of our beautiful human jigsaw puzzle. Without everyone, we would have surely failed.

Several companies also chipped in with materials, equipment, advice and ground support. They did so without expecting payment, without asking any questions and with great enthusiasm.

The collaboration between individuals and corporations, comprising everyone from design engineers to satellite surveyors, drone pilots to welders, is a testament to the power of kindness.

When kind people come together, when they cooperate and collaborate with understanding, respect and the greater good in mind, truly miraculous things can be achieved.

CHAPTER EIGHTEEN

MIRACLES CAN HAPPEN

In the final days of the rescue, a senior commander in the Indian military invited me for a cup of tea and biscuits in a secluded spot on top of the mountain. Just the two of us were sitting up there. A small dispatch had been sent ahead to set up a small camp table with a white linen tablecloth, tea for two and biscuits.

I remember my utter dismay at the scene. It looked like something out of the television show *M*A*S*H*. Me, wearing my King Gee shirt and Aldi high-vis workwear, and him decked out head-to-toe in a battlefield uniform.

'I think it seems to be going OK,' he told me between sips of his English Breakfast. It felt more like a question than an observation.

I nodded, biting into a biscuit. 'It is, but we need to stay calm and focused.'

He watched me deeply for a few moments in quiet

contemplation before giving a single gentle nod. He threw the remnants of his cup onto the trunk of a tree.

'Good.'

And with that, our meeting was over. He was satisfied that things were running as well as they could be.

The level of concern, the extent of empathy shown by the army guys, was touching. As senior officers from more privileged parts of the country, they (like me) did not really have much in common with the workers. They had different lives and experiences, far removed from each other. A few generations back, they might not have given too much thought to the fate of those at the bottom of the caste system.

But now? It felt like things were transforming rapidly in real time. These men of status deeply cared. They seemed truly proud to be part of the rescue. They were fighting for their countrymen, determined to bring them home safely.

And now, in a quiet and polite meeting with a random pink Australian who had a shirt pocket full of flowers, one of the highest figures in the defence force was showing that same kind of beautiful care.

'We just need to believe we can,' I told the military bigwig, before he left to begin the descent to the rescue site. 'We need to imagine the future we want and then make it happen.'

He paused and peered at me. Then he smiled.

'I believe.' And with that, he was off.

I have come to refer to my thought process during the rescue as 'imagineering'. Some more spiritually inclined people may refer to it as 'manifestation', but I reckon what I do is a little more involved than simple wishful thinking.

Let me explain.

The first step in imagineering is to have a clear picture in your mind of how you want something to be. Imagine the end point and the outcome. Do not ask *how* you will achieve something. Just picture how it will be *when* you do, not if. Settle on the future you want, believe it can happen and work your way backwards from there.

Make it happen. Just do it. You cannot ever hope to walk on water if you are afraid to get wet. Take a step into the ocean. Have a crack and see what happens.

Just do stuff. That is my philosophy.

It sounds weird. Fellow scientists and extremely rational thinkers who might be reading these words have probably just rolled their eyes almost out of their sockets.

But that is how I think about it.

I did not arrive at that mountain, look at the situation and ask myself how the hell we were going to get those men out. I never once allowed myself to think about how it is usually so rare that anyone survives these kinds of disasters. I did not let myself ponder the *how* at all until much later.

I imagineered a scenario where those forty-one kids emerged through the wall of rock and dirt alive, uninjured and safe. I pictured a reality where that was achieved without anyone on our side being injured or worse. I saw everyone working together and believing wholeheartedly in the unbelievable to get it done.

And then I worked backwards.

When I look back at the vision from that time, at all those media reports from the site, I feel like I am watching a totally different person on the screen. He looks like me, he sounds like me and parts of him are deeply familiar. But he is so in the zone, so calm and collected, that he could be medicated.

I was in that zone the whole way through the rescue.

I do not know whether it is intuition or professional expertise, or an uncomfortable combination of both, but I've had cause to listen to my gut more than a few times in my life.

For instance, there was the tunnel project in Albania, the one where those unfriendly people tried to kill me. Every single day of that job, I listened to the mountain to get a sense of whether we were going to be safe or if we should retreat.

The Albanian government was pushing hard for the tunnel to open before the election. But on the day of a special 'trial drive' for interested locals, the tunnel operators fled. They packed their bags in the dead of night and left town without saying a word. They had been threatened by locals, who felt they better deserved the lucrative contract for running the tunnel post-completion.

On the preview day, the only option was for Gail and me to take one side of the tunnel each and keep a close eye on things.

'See you when I see you,' I said gingerly, as I drove off in a dual-cab ute.

At our respective ends, alongside the police, we checked vehicles queuing to enter the tunnel for bombs. We monitored sensitive safety indicators for any signs of movement. We carefully worked to get each car through to appease the government while balancing safety responsibilities.

It was exhausting. The government expected some 2000 vehicles would come to check out the tunnel on this special opening day. In reality, it was more than 10,000. Forty vehicles would travel in a convoy with a safety car and fire engine leading the way.

After four days, Gail and I were reunited. Both of us were as close to broken as we have ever been.

Not long after this so-called 'grand opening' and in the shadow of the election, which the ruling government had won, a fifty-metre-long section of the tunnel collapsed.

Two weeks earlier, my gut had told me that we had to get out of there. Something felt wrong. Really wrong. I could sense that the mountain was trying to tell me that it was unhappy. It wanted us to leave, and to leave now.

I demanded the whole team evacuate. I blew the whistle and we downed tools. This decision made some people angry. They could not understand why I was seemingly comfortable one day then almost terrified the next. But I dug my heels in. When the tunnel caved in, they understood that I was right.

By then, the election was won and the Prime Minister's Office was not too fussed about getting things up and running again. So I wrote a report, Gail and I packed our bags, and we flew home to Australia. We did not return. It was more than a year until the tunnel finally reopened.

Because of my decision, there was no loss of life during the collapse. On reflection, there are distinct parallels with the India rescue. It felt miraculous that my instincts had been so strong, and no-one was killed.

Another time in my life when trusting my gut led to a fairly significant outcome involved my now-wife, Divina.

She was a waitress in Doha at a US chain restaurant called TGI Fridays. I would often go in there to eat because, like all foreign fast-food or diner-style outlets, the food was consistent, affordable and reliable.

Divina and I would chat whenever I was in. We had an instant rapport. The first time we met, her warmth of heart struck me the moment she came to my table to take my order.

As time passed, I peeled back the layers of her story, slowly uncovering the remarkable person she is. Like me, she carried a fire for people – a deep, unshakable commitment to helping others. Her journey began in the Philippines, where she trained to become a midwife. Not for the prestige or for personal gain, but because she wanted to make a difference.

But life has a way of crushing dreams, and hers came in the form of unpaid exam fees. It wasn't her lack of skill or dedication that held her back, but the simple fact that she couldn't afford to get her exam results released.

Her family's situation was a tangled mess, burdened by debt that seemed to grow with every passing day. So, like countless others searching for hope, she set her sights overseas. From 2008 to 2018, she worked in Dubai, Singapore and finally Qatar, each new city with a new contract. Each contract offered new hope, trying to carve out a better life, not for herself, but for her family back home.

But the reality of being an overseas worker was far from the dream she had envisioned. Much of the money she earned disappeared – stolen through slick, well-practised frauds pulled off by corrupt employers and labour agents. Yet, despite all the setbacks and hardships, she never let her spirit falter. Instead, she redirected her energy into something even more powerful – helping her fellow Filipino expatriates who were struggling, just like her. In Qatar, where so many faced the same difficulties, Divina gave whatever she could, offering support, comfort and kindness. It's just who she is. She couldn't walk away, even when the odds were stacked against her.

Divina is a born humanitarian. We bonded over our shared passions, especially for kindness and our belief that it can be a powerful force for good.

She was a hard worker. That much was clear. So I decided to bring her into my team. I hired her as a part-time safety officer in my company in addition to her full-time job. We worked closely together. She trained in construction and underground safety, so we became almost attached at the hip.

For a time, my daughter Hannah came to work with me in Qatar. I do not know how I missed it at the time, but now I realise she had an ulterior motive of sorts.

By that stage, I had been unmarried for almost a decade and Hannah decided it was time I met someone. I was long overdue to have another crack at love, she argued. So, being analytical and evidence-based, she created an Excel spreadsheet of all the women in my life.

She assigned various attributes and characteristics to each of them, and cross-correlated those with my various strong points and flaws, to be frank – to calculate who was most likely to be a good match.

Divina came out on top.

'Take her on a date,' I was instructed.

I am fairly conservative when it comes to courtship. Boring, some may say. Hannah would probably describe me that way. Chasing a woman like some kind of Lothario was definitely not my style. I could not hope to pull it off.

I also felt like one long and turbulent marriage was more than enough for one lifetime. I planned on dying single. No part of me had imagined another person – a wife – being in my life ever again.

But something in my gut told me to give this a go at least. I relented. Divina and I went on a date, which in itself was quite risky in a country like Qatar. She was an unwed woman, I was a single guy, so simply going out together was not something that was looked upon fondly. We had to be careful.

Divina was quite suspicious of me, I think. A lot of men with bad motives are in countries like Qatar, especially among those pursuing a foreign woman.

It probably helped ease her mind that I looked like the least desirable single guy in all of Qatar. I dressed terribly, I did not have any flashy jewellery and I drove a bomb of a car. Despite all that, even though I was definitely not a catch, she decided she would like to go out and have a pizza with me.

Then she decided to see me a second time, a third time and a fourth time.

We got on really well, but took things very slowly. We 'dated' in a casual, no-pressure way for probably six months or more. As we grew closer, I could no longer imagine an existence where she was not by my side.

When she first came home with me to the farm at Monbulk, it was as if the sun had decided to shine brighter, just for us. The place felt different – alive in a way it never had before, and that was entirely because of her. The air seemed fresher, the grass greener, and there was this warm, gentle glow that wrapped itself around the house and spilled down into the fields.

Make no mistake, she left her mark on the place too. The house now sports a vibrant red chimney and a bold splash of lime green – a true reflection of Divina's style. Any trace of the old 'snobby home beautiful' aesthetic or Laura Ashley pretentiousness was well and truly wiped out, replaced by something far more colourful, a far more real. Far more *her*.

Even with all my stuff jammed inside it, the house had often felt empty. Unless the kids were visiting, it was just me, most of the time. A fairly lonely and transient experience. A place where I rested only when I had to, usually between trips to far-flung places.

Now, it felt like a home. Our home. It has become a very happy place in the years since, thanks to Divina.

In 2023, eight years after meeting each other in slightly strange circumstances, and cementing our relationship with the help of my daughter Hannah and an Excel spreadsheet, Divina and I got married.

Being married to me cannot be an easy proposition. I mean, you have read this far, so surely you would agree. My life can be chaotic and I am not a small, demure personality. But I feel accepted and backed in a way I never have before.

Divina has never questioned what I do and the sometimes manic, often unpredictable way I work. Even when the stakes are high, she is supportive. Throughout the India rescue, she never complained about the risks I was taking, how long I had been away from home or our inability to stay in regular contact. She saw that I was trying to do something important and felt just as strongly about getting those forty-one kids home to their families.

Every so often, when my phone would connect to a dim cellular signal from afar, my screen would light up with messages from Divina. They were loving and encouraging – kind words of support, reminding me to believe in myself and not lose hope.

More and more water was dripping from the roof. That's never a good sign. And more and more rocks were falling into the rescue zone. Weeks had gone by since the collapse and, as one media outlet bluntly put it, rescuers 'had little to show for it'.

Steel rings were fabricated and erected to strengthen the rescue zone – a series of pipes were laid on the tunnel floor. If the tunnel blew while we were in the rescue zone, the aim was to try to scramble into a pipe for sanctuary and refuge. The convergence data (survey and drone-based light detection and ranging [LiDAR]) was showing asymmetric convergence in the rescue zone. The tunnel was collapsing – collapsing on us.

Our auger had been making decent progress, until it stopped. It hit a giant pile of bent and broken steel – huge chunks of the reinforcements from the roof of the tunnel that had come down in the collapse.

Think of it as trying to get through a sandpit with a teaspoon and suddenly hitting a buried car. We could not dig through the mountain collapse equivalent of a Toyota Corolla with a simple piece of cutlery.

Everything had gone to shit. Nothing was working. There was a potent sense that we had run out of options. The media were hounding me. Everyone was utterly exhausted, having worked around the clock for weeks only to wind up nowhere.

At a time when we had lost so much – machinery and backup plans – we were losing the most important thing we had. Hope.

What could I do to lift spirits? Could I make some kind of gesture, akin to praying at the temple, that might inspire everyone to keep pushing? To not lose faith?

I had an idea. It involved finding a yellow hardhat to wear.

I told a friend my plan. I wanted to get rid of my white hardhat, signifying that I was a manager and not a yellow hardhat-wearing worker. From now on, I would only wear a yellow one. He liked it, but upped the ante. He knew the boss of *all* the yellow hats, so he came up with a way I could incorporate him, too.

My friend would swap the big boss's hat for a new yellow one. He would bring me the real deal and I would take it somewhere special. All going well, its return would be well-received and we could all bond in a way that lifted morale.

We could all be on the same team, fighting the same fight, still believing in the same audacious goal. The big boss with his yellow hat. His workers with their yellow hats. The forty-one trapped men with theirs.

And me with mine.

My friend smiled. A grin spread across my face. We shook on the plan and agreed to meet at the tunnel entry at dawn. Dawn was in four hours – we had made our plan while inspecting the geophones on top of the mountain at night.

At dawn, we converged on the tunnel portal and, by chance, the exact moment we arrived the big boss of the miners was coming out. We swapped the big boss's yellow hat for mine – I got it.

In possession of the big boss's hat, I went to the makeshift temple, which was in a concrete pipe out the front of the tunnel, and met with two priests. I asked them if they would bless the hat. They agreed enthusiastically. One holy man anointed it with various oils and powders while the other chanted prayers alongside him.

With his pinkie finger, one of the priests painted a red swastika on the front of it. Now, of course, this ancient Hindu symbol has nothing to do with Nazi Germany. It has been a feature of Hinduism, Jainism and Buddhism for thousands of years – long before an evil Western regime hijacked it.

The swastika symbolises the sun and is a sign of good luck and prosperity. The word itself stems from the Sanskrit words *su*, meaning 'good', and *asti*, referring to 'wellbeing and good fortune'. It is included in prayers within Hinduism's oldest scriptures, the *Rig Veda*.

In 1920, Adolf Hitler stole the symbol, rotated it forty-five degrees, removed some dots and declared it to be the official emblem of the Nazi Party. For much of the world, the awful connotations of that brutal period of human history have tainted the symbol ever since, but Hindus, Buddhists and Jains are not willing to let it go. And rightly so.

So it was that day when a yellow hardhat received a blessing outside a tunnel high in the Himalayas.

I put the blessed yellow hat on my head and went back inside the tunnel. That lifted everyone's spirits enormously. It was a symbolic shift – that there was still hope and we just had to seize it. The team drew extra energy from this to push on and refocus on the outcome we wanted.

I had also demonstrated that I was a white hat no more. I was firmly a yellow hat, in the trenches with them. Committed. Determined. Hopeful.

Down in the welding area, it was all hands on deck. Soldiers, tunnel fabricators and volunteers were working side by side, designing and building rescue equipment out of whatever scraps we could find. When your only tool is a welder, suddenly everything looks like a job for 10-millimetre plate steel. I found myself right there with them – helping design, weld and inspect the rescue cart and steel rings. Colin 'Col', the kind TAFE teacher from Warburton, had voluntarily taught me how to weld during the chaos of Covid, and now, in some strange twist of fate, that kindness was just another piece in the impossible jigsaw of this rescue.

I felt sure we were almost there. We were close to success, I could feel it. I felt that the mountain was telling me as much, too.

A hard-nosed betting man would have steered clear of this particular gamble, however. Even the most reckless punter would look at the cards he had been dealt and walk away, folding because the odds were so shocking.

The tried-and-tested tools to cut through rock had failed. We had rolled out the biggest and toughest machine possible, certain it could defeat the aftermath of the mountain's fury. Even that promptly blew up. We had exhausted most of our options and torn through the equipment at our disposal.

In the end, all we had left were our hands. History's first tool, doing what a technologically advanced and expertly engineered machine could not. We decided to use those humble human tools to scrape back rock, rubble and dirt bit by bit, about 100 millimetres at a time.

And with our hands we had to excavate the last 10 metres – or, as I said live to 1.3 billion viewers, just the last 1000 millimetres or so.

A pipe, measuring about eighty centimetres in diameter, was drilled into the debris as far as we could get it. Two men would crawl in with a trolley about two metres long. They would load clumps of rock and dirt into it by hand. Then they would pull the trolley back out on a rope by hand and empty it, before sending it back in.

It was a slow and painstaking operation. But with each load we removed, the pipe could be pushed a little bit closer to where the forty-one men were trapped.

Each time the trolley was pulled back with a load of rubble, it was a reminder of just how unstable the situation was. It was rock, but barely. The shards had begun to turn to dust just by being scraped up in a worker's hands and thrown into the trolley.

I still have all my notes from the rescue. They are in a bright red notebook that I carried with me, in which I sketched out the mechanics of the process that would allow us to free the men.

It covers just three pages. That is it – the solution in its entirety. It is a rudimentary sketch of our slow-and-steady approach to reaching the forty-one men on the other side of the pile of rubble.

But it is a reminder of the time a team of people, propelled by belief and determination, worked together to design and build a metal cart that would save people's lives.

We could never have done it without courageous and determined men, who many might have had a tendency to deride.

In India, a special group of men who work underground are known as 'rat-hole miners'. I do not love the term, I have to admit. It severely underplays not just the significance of the work they do, but also their expertise.

But that is how they are known in India. In a society famed for its deeply entrenched social hierarchy, these men are at the very bottom of the ladder. Or more accurately, they were never on the ladder to start with.

But now, after the events of late 2023, they are regarded by many as heroes.

Twelve of these men proved integral in the rescue operation. Without them, without their dedication and their bravery, I cannot imagine how things might have played out. I cannot begin to fathom how much longer it might have taken to get to the trapped miners, or if we would have succeeded at all.

Rat-hole miners are part of a small group of workers who hand-dig tunnels, clear blocked sewerage pipes and crawl through them to excavate coal with their bare hands. It is so dangerous that some parts of India forbid this type of mining. In the decade before the bans were implemented, human rights groups estimated as many as 225 rat-hole miners had been killed on the job. That's twenty-three a year for ten years. Unbelievable.

Given how poorly the men are paid, however, some unscrupulous mining operators see it as a cost-effective solution that is impossible to resist. And so the practice carries on in secret in many parts of the country.

These men come from the poorest regions of India. They have been recruited because of their short stature, and are paid as little as five dollars a day (twice as much as the trapped tunnellers) for their backbreaking and hugely risky work.

Inside the tunnel, forming the core of our rescue mission, these men very softly excavated rock by hand, which allowed us to push the pipe a little further forward. It was painstaking and precarious, but it had to be. They were part of our 'go soft' approach, which was crucial if we were to avoid pissing off the mountain any further.

Two men at a time crawled deep inside the eighty-centimetre-diameter pipe, working in four-hour shifts.

What they did took enormous courage. We knew of the huge risk involved with the process and they understood it, too.

In the moments before they broke through to the area where the men were trapped, I assembled the rescue team and had a quiet and calm conversation with them.

'If you get in there and there's another collapse, run away. Don't try to get back into the tunnel we've just dug. Move to the very back of the space. I'll come and get you.

'We won't give up. We won't leave. I'll come back for you.

'When I promised that we'd get these men out without anyone getting hurt, I meant *everyone*. That includes you.'

They had to trust us. They had to know we had their backs and that we cared.

In the hours before they broke through, I remember someone remarking that we should have been through by now. The feeling was that progress had been slower than hoped. The men should have been reached by now.

'It's OK,' I smiled. 'The mountain has not collapsed. The men are safe. We are making progress.'

When one of the rat-hole miners eventually broke through to the cavern where the men were trapped, I am told it was a scene of jubilation. One miner ran forward to embrace his rescuer in a warm hug. Another few burst into tears. Their nightmare was finally over.

After seventeen long and gruelling days, at around 8.50 pm on 28 November, the first of those forty-one men crawled out of the metal pipe. The rescue crew erupted into cheers. That excited scene was repeated forty more times until the very last trapped worker had emerged.

We had done it. They were free.

I was not in front of the cameras, though I could have been. Just moments earlier, I stood with the dignitaries, waiting in the triage area deep inside the tunnel. But as the rescuers went in, I stepped back – choosing instead to sit behind the families of the trapped men, with my back against the tunnel wall, my hands resting on the rocks. My job was done; this was their moment. The celebration wasn't mine to intrude upon with my pink face splashed across international TV.

I watched the families as the news came. Their reactions weren't what I had expected. While the rescue teams were cheering, the families were silent – almost as if they were seeing ghosts. Forty-one men had come home safe, and not one person was injured.

To see the look in the eyes of the rescued men, to see their beaming smiles one by one, forty-one times, was one of the most rewarding moments in my life. It was the very best of humanity at work. It was a thing of beauty.

'Christmas has come early,' I told one waiting reporter.

Each of the workers were rushed to a hospital in Chinyalisaur, some thirty kilometres away, for medical treatment. Miraculously, all the men were in good health and high spirits. They were kept for observation but the remarkable reality was that everyone was fine.

The rescue site and surrounding village broke out in celebration. India's largest-ever rescue operation had been a success. The impossible was made possible. No-one could quite believe it. The scenes were fittingly festive.

Or at least, that is what I have been told. I quietly slunk away the first moment I could, disappearing into the shadows.

CHAPTER NINETEEN

AN UNCOMFORTABLE TRUTH

A huge amount of science and engineering was involved in bringing those forty-one men out of the rubble to safety, but the fact remains that the outcome was . . . dare I say it, miraculous.

Not long after leaving the tunnel following the rescue, I was pounced on by a camera crew. To watch it back now is quite unbelievable. I am almost floating. I am so elated and bright, despite being exhausted. You could have knocked me over with a feather.

'You've just witnessed a miracle,' I told the reporter. That is truly how it felt in the moment. It is still kind of how it feels now.

The uncomfortable truth is that I did things in the months before the rescue that do not make any sense. They barely made sense then, and they don't now, in spite of each seeming to have happened for a very good reason. Thinking about it, I find myself even more confused.

Why did I pack my rescue gear? Why did I decide to bring two weeks' worth of tinned tuna on an international study tour, which I ended up living on during the rescue? It is really odd. It is hard to comprehend those major coincidences.

My whole manner changed before the rescue. By the time it came about, my frame of mind was in the absolute best place it could be to perform in the calmest and most in-tune state possible.

As I write this, I have three red strings tied around my right wrist. One was tied on by the priests at the temple at the entrance to the tunnel. Another one was given to me at the top of the mountain as I gave thanks after the rescue. The third was gifted to me at a Hindu temple here in Melbourne.

I was told to keep them on, not to remove them, until they naturally fall away on their own at some point in the future. When they fail I'm told to be reminded of the inevitability of death.

And that is what I will do.

The only problem is that I lost a fair stack of weight during the rescue, eating tins of tuna and not much else. Since being home and celebrating with the help of all kinds of delicious and fattening foods, those bracelets are getting a bit tight.

Recently, I appeared on a podcast hosted by spiritualist and academic Professor BC Anant, who founded the organisation BCA Bharat some fifteen years ago. As he puts it, the group aims to bridge the gap between the Hindu-Vedic era and the present-day technological and industrial era.

We spoke a lot about the things I felt during and after the tunnel rescue. I explained my inner conflict about things that cannot be explained with science. Things that seem to verge on the spiritual, which is not a phrase I would have used not too long ago.

I spoke to him about how tuned in I felt during the rescue. I kept framing it that way – as being tuned in to the world around me. A hyper-focus on the human, natural and spiritual elements of the operation.

He described the sensation as being 'connected', rather than tuned in. Everything happens for a reason, he said, and I was a big part of the reason for the successful outcome. For whatever reason, the gods had blessed me. They had shone their favour upon me and, as a result, I had become connected to the place, and those forty-one men, in a deep way.

While we were talking, he began to tear up. Tears were welling in his eyes as I explained how I was feeling and my inner turmoil, about how unusual and foreign things have felt in the time since the rescue.

For him, what I was describing is not unusual at all. I was describing how he feels about the world and how he views life. It was a religious experience. He understood perfectly why we achieved the impossible. He completely got what had happened.

It was a religious miracle that is bigger than my capacity to reason with science.

Every person, every rock and piece of dirt, everything in that place played its role perfectly. Not out of chance or because of some random coincidence, but thanks to the gods. We were all where we were meant to be. Everything was in its perfect place.

A lot about this sits uncomfortably with me. It is so outside of my normal way of thinking that I almost do not recognise the person writing these words.

And yet, I am totally fascinated by it. I am determined to dig into the unknown in a bid to discover more. And when you think about it, that is the role of a scientist – to explore and discover.

To simply shrug it off and reject it would make me narrow-minded. It would mean I have blinkers on and refuse to look at other conclusions.

I have thought a lot about religion and spirituality in the time since the rescue. I have spoken about it to people, both those of faith and not, more now than I ever have in my entire life.

Still, I don't feel overly qualified to come to any concrete resolution. While a lot of what I felt during the rescue was odd, the outcome itself was odd, too. How did I get my head into that particular space? How did I take myself somewhere that is so foreign to me?

I decided to spend some time examining it through a lens that is much more comfortable for me to peer through. Science.

I began to explore some of the branches of quantum physics.

A regular theme in my life has been a deep pondering of consciousness. I do not really understand what makes us different from other animals. I cannot come to terms with the fact that we are special as a species but without many clues as to why.

If you accept that we human beings have the power to make choices, and I certainly do, then that means I can create a particular future. I have the ability within certain unknown boundaries to make a future. That is the whole point of being alive – our ability to have the imagination to foresee a particular outcome then work towards it.

We can drive the outcome in a particular direction so we can get to a particular future, which then becomes the present.

It is a powerful thought. If that is true, and we extend the thought to make it even bigger, then how we think actually does impact the future.

It is like when you are in a rough patch in your life. You might be feeling a bit depressed or melancholy. The more you lean into that feeling, the more you accept it. As you absorb more and more of the negative feelings and thoughts, the darker those clouds get, and the more likely you will wind up in that future, I think. You choose to take those feelings on board and you drive yourself towards the darkness.

Let me put it this way. When teaching a teenager how to drive, a good driving instructor will tell them not to look at the potholes. If you stare at a pothole you are hurtling towards, you almost certainly will drive straight into it. Every single time. Instead, you look at the bitumen without a pothole.

You focus your energy on the place you want to be, not on the obstructions. Look to where you want to go. It kind of makes it happen.

I increasingly wonder if there is a realm of physics that actually fits this model. That is the world I want to be a part of. I want to live in a society where everyone gets together, decides we are not going to do this nasty and destructive shit anymore, and imagines a different future.

In the latest work in quantum physics, there is a co-operation among anaesthetists and doctors, mathematicians and physicists, and philosophers. Quite an eclectic grouping of people, to say the least. But they have all come together to try and understand what happens when someone is anaesthetised.

That fact is quite scary in itself – anaesthetists still do not fully understand what is going on when they put someone under anaesthetic. It feels like death. You do not slip off into a gentle slumber, have some dreams and wake up feeling like you have emerged from a restful sleep. It is simply nothing, a great nothingness. Something is, then it ceases to exist, and then it resumes. No-one in medicine is sure why that is or how exactly it works.

Let that be a comforting thought the next time you find yourself in a surgical theatre.

The latest theory is that we have quantum receptors inside the human brain. If this hypothesis is right, these quantum receptors are responsible for consciousness. And if *that* is true, then it means everything is connected, no matter how far apart it is.

In the quantum world, things can happen all at once. When a little packet of energy comes from the sun and lands on a leaf, for it to be converted into food for the plant, it has to find a pathway at a subcellular level. It has long been known that the process that occurs, photosynthesis, is far too efficient to be realistic. Something weird is going on. It is just too perfect.

Nano physicists believe that, at a quantum level, each little packet of energy coming from the sun simultaneously examines a million different options to move through the plant and picks the best one. Photosynthesis, the most important process for life as we know it, has a signature of quantum behaviour.

Why is that important? Because if we have got quantum receptors in our brains, it means that you and I are connected – if we can figure out how to tune in. It also means that Arnold was connected to the Himalayas and a group of forty-one total strangers trapped on the other side of a mammoth pile of rock.

If that is the case, it could explain consciousness as well as intuition. It could even explain how some people seem lucky and others do not. It could explain the sense of place so many of us feel.

It could explain my long sense of awe and attachment to the sun – the source of all energy, the lifeblood for everything living as we know on earth. In a moment, both sides of me – the scientist and the awakening spiritual self – could be in harmony together, in a way I hadn't imagined possible. They might no longer be at odds; they could be part of the same story.

And it could explain religion itself. It could explain *all* religions simultaneously. As in, they are all correct – they all merge at a quantum level because they are connected. Whether your sense of spirituality comes from Jesus,

Muḥammad, Buddha or whoever else, it would not matter anymore because there is a connection. Each religion describes a connection to the universe, to creation.

If that were to be the case – and who knows if we will find out in our lifetimes – it would be utterly upending. On the one hand, it is an incredibly unifying discovery, but on the other, it completely disables whole systems and dogmas. *Everyone* would be right, and I suspect a number of people would not want that to be the case.

Maybe there is science behind the inexplicable. Maybe there is a reason I arrived at the mountain in a particular state of mind, why I started listening to unusual music, why I started thinking and speaking in poetry, why I embarked on a world tour to collect all the knowledge and materials I needed to successfully execute an impossible mission. Maybe I was tuning in. I just did not realise what I was tuning in to.

I am not resolved on any of this stuff. I am yet to land on a position about what the hell happened – what was going on with me – that gives me closure. There is much I still cannot explain, and maybe I never will be able to.

I'm ready to have faith in this God of everything – of us all – based in science.

In the end, our hearts are what won this. You simply cannot engineer without some heart. On the flipside, I do not think you can have a successful humanitarian response without specialist expertise. You need both.

CHAPTER TWENTY

THE BOYS' BUBBLERS

As a man of a certain age, recently I have started casting my mind back. I have caught myself reflecting on my life, from childhood to now, in a bid to figure out what makes me tick. Why I am the way I am.

Why did I throw away a lucrative and successful law firm career? Why did I choose to go out on my own and take jobs based on the heart, rather than a cash-driven head? Why am I so willing to get on a plane to venture halfway around the world to be helpful, for free?

In the tapestry of human experience, each thread tells a story. My story is woven from the fibres of justice and fairness. My unshakable sense of what is right has fundamentally shaped who I am, in such a way that young Arnold might not recognise large parts of who I am now.

Don't get me wrong, he was hardly a selfish prick. He certainly had within him a whole set of admirable qualities. They just were not quite fully formed, and he had no way of guessing where they might end up taking him. I doubt he fully appreciated how he would become directed by a simmering sense of justice.

For me, it is not just about reacting to wrongs. It is about proactively striving for fairness and equity in every aspect of life. But it must be said, this principle has been both a source of strength and a challenging burden. My bank account could stand to be a bit more buoyant.

Growing up, I was acutely aware of the disparity between what was right and what was actually happening around me. At one of the schools I went to, there was this absolute arsehole of a bully who plagued the playground. No-one liked him. Everyone feared him. He was merciless.

This little shit's favourite thing to do was flog other kids' lunches. He would skulk around, peering at what everyone had in their lunchboxes, then strike. He snatched anything remotely delicious out of your hands, knocked the rest of it onto the ground and ran off laughing maniacally.

God help anyone who happened to be in possession of chocolate milk. This bully loved chocolate milk. He would carefully watch the canteen line to see who was buying one, then when out of teachers' view, he would claw it from you.

This guy fascinated and enraged me. I began observing him, looking for patterns, and identified a few pretty quickly. The big one was that he was predictable. His modus operandi was always the same. He never changed his approach and it became simple to anticipate his next move.

One day, I fished an empty chocolate milk container out of the bin and discreetly hid it in the bushes outside the toilet block. The next day at recess, I retrieved it without anyone seeing, crept into the loo and pissed in it. Outside in the playground, I made a show of having a delicious chocolate milk to enjoy. The bully took the bait hook, line and sinker.

Importantly, the bully did not so much as pause as he drank my rancid milk and piss cocktail. I had expected a beating, but got none. He did not even flinch. It taught me that bullies must save face too – yet another weird lesson in life.

Did the punishment fit the crime? At the time, I thought so. It was an extreme measure to take, I admit, but even little Arnold could not accept people being treated horribly and unfairly without doing something. Like a red cloth waved to a bull, I was programmed to speak up. Those unjust moments sparked a fire within me.

I started to question the status quo well before I even knew what 'status quo' meant. As a kid, I would see a situation that did not feel equitable and figure out a way to address it. Demanding better, not just for myself but for others, seemed like a perfectly natural thing to do.

Some of the adults I encountered, however, did not agree.

I have a vivid memory of organising a campaign to fix the boys' bubblers at one of my primary schools. They call them something different in each Australian state, I think. Water fountains. Drink taps. When I was a kid, they were bubblers.

And the boys' bubblers at school were an absolute mess. They barely worked and were absolutely filthy with rust and bits of dirt. The flow was so weak that you basically had to put your mouth over the whole thing to get any water. By comparison, the girls were drinking out of the bubbler equivalent of the Trevi Fountain.

I felt it was unfair that the bubblers were maintained differently; that there was clearly one standard for girls and another for boys. I mean, the fact that the school had gendered sources of water at all is pretty absurd in hindsight.

But I felt it was a pretty clear indication of the lack of care shown to one group over another. Girls were nice and boys were gross. Maybe I was off the mark, but that is certainly how it seemed to little Arnold.

I was pissed off. I wanted a drink of water and getting one was a real hassle. So I created a petition and had all the boys in the school sign it. When I presented it to the front office, I thought I might be commended for taking some initiative.

I got in deep shit instead. They were so angry that I would dare to suggest any kind of unequal treatment at school. In the end, the taps got fixed and everyone had an abundant supply of water, regardless of sex. That is a win in my book.

As I grew older, this sense of justice became more than a personal value. It evolved into a principle that guided my professional and personal interactions.

Gail has often remarked that I take everyone at face value. I do not judge. I want to believe that all the people I encounter have good hearts and pure intentions. I will give you the benefit of the doubt. But break my trust or lie to me, and we are finished.

I cannot stomach being lied to. I have dumped a few clients in the past, regardless of tenure or professional fee, after discovering they had misled or deceived me.

Of course, I understand that few things, if any, in life are black and white. Almost everything we do, everything that happens to us, is made up of important context and background. Things are rarely simple and clear cut.

I get that. I get that human beings are highly fallible, and I am no exception. We are driven by a potent cocktail of emotions, some of which can be irrational or illogical. It is easy to misread a situation or overreact to a set of circumstances. And hell, the way we are wired from childhood, thanks to a delightful mix of nature and nurture, determines how we view the world, how we interact with each other, and the kind of response we are likely to have to a situation.

What you believe, how you see things, what makes you tick, could be totally different from how I engage with the world.

But overall, my main guiding principle is pretty simple – don't be a dickhead. Don't hurt anyone, don't be nasty. Just be nice to people. That's about it.

One of the most profound lessons I have learned is that justice is a journey, not a destination. The world is in a constant state of change, and new challenges and inequalities emerge over time. Sometimes, it seems as though we are repeating history or slipping back into the past, losing a bit of the positive ground we have claimed. I do not know about you, but I have been feeling that way a lot recently . . .

I suppose a powerful reminder is that the fight for fairness is not a one-time effort, but an ongoing process of learning, adapting and advocating. This means that, even as we make progress, there is always more work to be done. We need to stay vigilant and committed, even when the path forward does not seem clear – and especially when progress seems slow.

My sense of justice is not just a characteristic; it is much more than that. And it is a double-edged sword, both a gift and a burden. It is a gift because it provides clarity and purpose, and it can be a burden because it requires constant effort and reflection.

I think I have done a reasonable job of instilling some of my values in my children. Justice. Working for the greater good. Sacrifice.

All my children know about disasters. When they were little, I made a point of taking them along with me on various jobs. Lots in Australia, even a few overseas. Each of them has seen up close the aftermath of something going wrong.

Sam, my eldest child, was alongside me helping with the Waterfall train crash at the start of 2003. On 31 January, a Tangara set G7 full of passengers departed Central Station in Sydney at 6.24 am, heading for Port Kembla via Wollongong.

At about 7.15 am, the driver suffered a heart attack and lost consciousness. The train was travelling at 117 kilometres an hour. As it approached a bend, the train's speed should have slowed considerably. Trains are meant to take curves like that at no more than sixty kilometres an hour. As a result, the train derailed.

It overturned and smashed into the rocky walls of a small tunnel cut into a hill. Two carriages landed on their side. Another pair were significantly damaged in the collision. Seven people were killed and scores more injured.

The investigation I assisted with found that the so-called 'deadman's brake', which is meant to kick in if the driver takes pressure off a mechanism in the event they become incapacitated or even momentarily distracted, had malfunctioned.

A geologist, Sam had worked with me on a job in the Middle East, too. He is a brilliant problem-solver and a rational and considerate guy. In the end, I think he had seen too much destruction and too much death. He wanted a change. These days, he works in banking.

Hannah, my second child, is an environmental geologist. She works as an engineer in tunnelling projects, so has kind of followed in my footsteps. We have worked together, closely, on several different jobs, including the Metro rail project in Doha.

Like Sam, I think she has tried to steer clear of the death and disaster side of things, preferring to work at the start of a project's lifespan. Her focus is on preventing the types of crises that I am called to. She has seen them since she was little and so her inspiration is to make sure, from the get-go, that nothing goes wrong.

Then there's Edward. He too came along to work with me a few times when he was little, but decided he wanted nothing to do with it. Instead, he studied technology and these days works in cloud-based data analytics. Everything he does is pretty cool.

In the year before I went off on my international study tour and the tunnel rescue, he announced he was going to marry the love of his life. She is an Indian girl from a conservative family in Pune, and took her degree at MIT Pune, which just so happens to also be where one of India's reputable Tunnel Courses is taught.

In early 2023, I took a trip to Pune to meet her family. They are the kind of family that might have preferred a marriage with a nice Indian boy of their choosing, not a computer nut from Australia. I tried to convince them with my presence to give their blessing to this unexpected union.

At the time, they were likely suspicious of me. But that has all changed since the rescue. I think I demonstrated that I am a decent person. Now, they treat me and Edward as honorary Indians. As I write this I am preparing to travel to India for their wedding. By the time you read this sentence maybe the universe will have blessed my family with Indian grandchildren.

Finally, there is my stepdaughter, Trisha. She goes to the local school here in Monbulk and is exceptionally good at mathematics, psychology and chemistry. She is so smart and caring. I am excited to see what she decides to do with her life, because there are endless possibilities. Right now, she aspires to be a nurse – someone who selflessly gives back, just like her mum.

CHAPTER TWENTY-ONE

THE LONG WAY HOME

The moment the last of the forty-one workers was freed, my cohort of rescuers headed back to the hotel to freshen up. There was not much point sticking around. The men had been rushed into ambulances and taken to hospital, so we were no longer needed.

On the way back to our accommodation, someone figured out it was someone's birthday. He had not said anything before – our focus was on the task at hand – but now that our duties were done, we had to celebrate this special occasion.

We staged an impromptu birthday party. Someone ran out to find flowers so they could be presented to the birthday boy. A cake was hastily organised from God knows where. The Indian version of the 'Happy Birthday' song was sung with great enthusiasm.

We each took turns feeding each other a mouthful of cake from a single spoon, which is apparently a common and popular custom on occasions like these.

A huge contingent of the press pack were there, too. After hearing the happy commotion from their rooms upstairs, they ventured down to see what was happening. They were just as exhausted as we were, but the jovial mood infected them, too. We were laughing and singing, shoulder-to-shoulder. After peppering me with questions about the rescue relentlessly every day for days, suddenly there was nothing more to be said.

It was hilarious. It was almost like we had forgotten this enormous and miraculous thing we had just achieved and moved on with our lives. Let's have a birthday party! Why not? I still cannot get over how surreal the whole thing felt.

One minute, we were underground pulling men to safety, and the next we found ourselves sitting in a modest hotel high up in the Himalayas feeding each other cake. I love it.

After the rescue, I was directed by officials to get on a helicopter to return to the city with them for a series of meetings, briefings and formalities. It was a directive rather than an invitation. I had to leave. There was also the risk of a happy mob forming, and taking souvenirs of me – some hair, a tooth, my clothes. Best I depart pronto.

That did not sit right to me. It did not seem appropriate to suddenly put my white hardhat back on and join the ranks of the executive, leaving those on the lower rungs of the ladder with whom I had bonded.

I also did not want to stick around and hog the spotlight. The men were out. India's children had been returned. My job was done.

By chance I met the Prime Minister's adviser in the hallway. I sought his counsel. He smiled and said, 'You know what you have to do'.

So I did a runner.

I went to the village to thank those who had given me flowers each day. I went to say goodbye to an elderly spiritual guru who, for the duration of the rescue mission, had positioned himself on a ridgetop partway up the mountain to pray and speak to the gods.

I then went to the tunnel and publicly declared a miracle had occurred to 1.3 billion people – if they were listening.

Then I trekked with the rescue workers to a temple on the mountaintop to give thanks. Two bells were rung, piercing the silence of the wilderness. I had felt compelled to make the journey to the mountaintop, to the high temple, alongside the State Disaster Response Fund rescue team. It was something I had to do – to give thanks, to show my gratitude to the mountain and to the goddess Kali for releasing those forty-one men, and for allowing us to do our jobs. We had been permitted to save those men, and none of us were harmed in the process. It felt that it was the least I could do in exchange for receiving exactly what I had asked for.

Away from the glare of the media, alone on the mountaintop and surrounded by the breathtaking enormity of nature, I sobbed. I thanked Kali for her mercy, thanked the mountain for working with us, and in a quiet moment, I even thanked myself – for finding the strength to contribute to this remarkable feat of human will and triumph.

On the way back, the men from the mighty Indian National Disaster Response Force brought the trekking group to a halt. We had come across an enormous fallen tree suspended above the path. They felt it was the perfect natural stage on which to spontaneously deliver a performance. It was a gleeful and soul-stirring song and dance of thanks.

I had no idea what they were singing, only that it was called the 'Arnold song' – a special composition the men created just for me. It was a touching moment. The emotion of it, the relief and elation you could see radiating from their fatigued bodies, brought a tear to my eye.

It also resonated with people in India. One of the men uploaded a clip of the performance to YouTube and Indian social media channels, where I am told it has since clocked up about 100 million views.

A small but vocal group of people within my organisation considered my conduct, in speaking so plainly with the press and making an emphatic promise of success, unacceptable for a president. Those individuals were so incensed that a formal complaint was made about my conduct and an inquiry into my fitness as president was launched. They questioned my behaviour.

I was contacted during the rescue – while those men were still trapped – and told I was behaving like a lunatic.

'What the hell do you think you're doing, Arnold?'

I didn't care. Forty-one kids on the other side of a massive pile of rocks needed us to believe that we could get to them.

They needed us to believe without question that they would be saved.

I was reminded that as President of ITA, I represent about 150,000 members from eighty-odd member nations across the globe. I was accused of tarnishing all their reputations, through my promise.

I resigned from my presidency of ITA on the spot – up there on the mountain.

The suggestion was that my behaviour was unbecoming and inappropriate for a scientist and an engineer, the organisation's president, no less. There was essentially a vote of no confidence and a probe of everything that I said and did during the India rescue.

The Indian authorities became aware that I had resigned and urged me to withdraw my resignation immediately. They explained there were deeper politics at play – things I hadn't fully grasped at the time. So I withdrew my resignation, and my withdrawal was accepted.

The internal investigation ultimately concluded that I had acted with the best of intentions and that the outcome was overwhelmingly positive. There would be no consequences to my leadership of the organisation, and no sanctions. The decency of the organisation I led outshone the loud voices of a few detractors.

But there had been warnings early on. Indian intelligence had quietly informed me during the rescue that personal attacks were inevitable. Dark, international politics were swirling around us, even as we were doing our best for humanity. And when the attacks came, they were brutal.

It's hard to put into words just how hurtful that experience was – not because of the accusations themselves, but because I had been forewarned. I knew this was coming. It wasn't about the rescue; it was about discrediting me as part of a larger political game.

It's a stark reminder that the battle between good and evil is very much alive, even here, high in the Himalayas, during what should have been a purely humanitarian mission.

For thousands of years, the great battles of good and evil have played out in these very mountains. The ancient Hindus recorded them in the Vedas. In some strange way, from the beginning, I *felt* it – I felt I had been caught up in a modern-day version of that ancient epic struggle between good and evil. I had played my part in a battle of the gods, a battle for humanity.

Forty-one lives were at stake. The situation was unpredictable and fast-changing. My professional opinion was that we had one way of getting them out alive, which was stepping outside the normal narrative and believing we could save them.

How dare those critics within my own organisation have a view of a situation when they were not there. It was such a cruel way to interrupt the situation and my behaviour – and worse, they were likely puppets.

There was a reason why I was saying things they might not necessarily expect me to say. I judged that the only way we could get these men out was to create a different future from the one everyone imagined was inevitable. We had to hijack reality and manipulate it into a future we wanted.

I am still really angry about it. I think it highlights how easily manipulated people are, and the motivations of small, narrow-minded and mean people. I am so disheartened that a small minority of people who respond so viciously to optimism and hope are within an organisation I lead. One drop of vinegar spoils the milk. Thankfully, most of my organisation are wonderful people – in fact, if you want to experience truly international cooperation and life-changing infrastructure through water, sewerage, transportation and power, come join ITA!

Of course there is also a simple explanation – maybe my critics were just jealous.

When I arrived at the airport to begin my long journey back to Australia, I was greeted by twenty-one beaming faces as I entered the terminal. Half of the group of rescued men were there, preparing to fly to their own homes and be reunited with their families. What are the chances?

I whipped out my phone, opened the camera app and hit Record. I quietly approached the group of wary workers. One spotted me and his eyes went wide, as though he had seen a ghost.

Or perhaps it was out of shock at the sight of me – a big, overgrown beard and wild hair after weeks with no access to basic personal grooming care.

The men looked around in confusion before their gazes settled on me. The realisation dawned. Somehow, we were face-to-face again when none of us suspected we ever would be.

One by one, they rushed forward to greet me with a tight handshake, beaming smile and gentle nod of the head.

'Thank you, sir,' they said over and over. 'Thank you. Thank you.'

This beautiful and emotional moment really drove home how lucky we all were.

I was in a reflective mood. I was a bit broken. Exhausted to an extent I have never experienced before and hope not to again any time soon. Despite that, I was happy. I felt proud.

I took to LinkedIn to share my own take on the Optimist's Creed. I wrote: 'As we build our tunnels – whatever be their goal – keep our eyes upon the rocks, and not upon the hole.'

Not long after returning to Monbulk, I received an adorable but surreal photograph of a fancy-dress day at Aditya Vidyashram Primary School in the coastal city of Puducherry in India's southeast.

There, on a stage in front of her teachers and peers, stood a girl of maybe seven or eight years old. She was dressed head-to-toe in fluorescent orange high-visibility pants and shirt, with a yellow helmet on her head and black work boots on her feet. She was a mini Arnold Dix. She had chosen to dress as me, inspired by what I had been a part of.

That right there was almost the highlight of the whole thing for me. Perhaps the greatest feeling in life is inspiring someone, particularly a child. Kids are so full of wonder and curiosity, untainted by the realities of life and the world, and their imaginations can take them anywhere and to everyone.

Despite this little girl's endless possibilities that day, of all the people she might have chosen, from celebrities and superheros to family members and social media stars, she picked me.

I reached out to her school and promised that, on my next visit to India, I would travel to Puducherry and visit. I can be her show-and-tell project. It's the least I can do.

My first return to India is for Edward's wedding. The date chosen – 12 November 2024 – is the anniversary of the collapse. I dared not mention it to them – another coincidence. After the wedding I'm heading back to the tunnel to give thanks again for the rescue. I suspect that in a very real sense I am now a pilgrim to the Himalayas to pay my respects to Baba Baukh Nag of that mountain tunnel and his superior – and my personal heroine – Maa Kali.

For the wedding my dress will be traditional orange and gold. The safety orange I have worn my entire professional life – the shirt I wore in the rescue – is EXACTLY the most auspicious colour for celebrating Kali – celebrating Indian style – celebrating life over death.

I have been asked a lot in the time since the rescue if there was anything I would do differently. The answer is simple. Nothing.

I do not know what might have happened if we had gone a centimetre to the left or right of where we dug. I do not know what tricks the mountain had up its sleeve, waiting to reveal. I have no clue what kind of difference a day, or even several hours, might have made.

And so having regrets is impossible.

I am happy that whatever we did turned out to be perfect. It was perfect because forty-one men were saved and no-one else got hurt. Not a single drop of blood.

And that never happens. Ever. This is the stuff of miracles.

EPILOGUE

In the aftermath of the tunnel rescue, a major investigation began to determine exactly what went wrong and how such a disaster could be prevented in the future.

Understandably, people's nervousness during the mission, followed by their joy at the incredible outcome, soon gave way to anger that the collapse had occurred in the first place.

A preliminary report released in December 2023 offered some damning findings, many of which I had suspected from early on.

For one, investigators were critical of the decision to run the tunnel along a shear zone, which is an area of rock that is highly deformed, quite thin and incredibly weak. They found that infrastructure authorities had not taken sufficient oversight over the placement of the tunnel.

Even though the tunnel was being dug at a shallow depth of about 140 metres, the environment was so unstable that it was put under extreme stress.

The region in the upper Himalayas is almost smack bang on top of a geological fault known as the Main Central Thrust. Here, the Indian Plate pushes under the Eurasian Plate, forming a volatile and constantly moving fault that runs for a few thousand kilometres from northwest to southeast.

Sensors and instruments should have been installed throughout the tunnel to offer early warnings about any instability. These could have provided vital data about the movement of the rock, allowing workers to take proper precautions.

The investigation also pointed out that during the digging process, several cavities had been found. That is, huge voids were present in the rock and revealed as digging carried on. This should have prompted engineers to install special supports and take greater care. The report found these cavities were crucial warning signs that were essentially ignored.

The absence of an escape tunnel, which could have provided a path to freedom in the event of a collapse, was also questioned in the preliminary report. I am not sure about that particular feature. I would prefer tunnels to be built right the first time.

Having said that, there is a practice in some Chinese tunnels to have a makeshift evacuation tube – I'm open minded.

The fact that twenty-one prior collapses had occurred without prompting a pause and major rethink was also criticised.

Each of the forty-one trapped workers received a financial settlement of two months' salary, a bonus of about A$5000. The government has issued the contractor of the tunnel with a show-cause notice, with speculation that criminal and civil proceedings are being considered.

Indian local media have since reported that the bill for the rescue, estimated to be up to A$1 million, will be copped by the contractor.

The Indian Ministry of Road Transport and Highways has committed to an overhaul of standard operating procedures. After the collapse and rescue, an audit of twenty-nine other tunnel projects currently underway across India was carried out to ensure proper practices were being followed and proper safety measures were in place.

Last week I met with Rahul Gupta – Chief Engineer of Road Tunnels of India in Sydney. He explained that the tunnel has been stabilised. The water is under control; the collapsing is in check. I've been welcomed back to the tunnel. It seems clear the pilgrims will get their safe link, avoiding the treacherous mountain pass.

I was not part of the investigation into what went wrong. In this instance, I am not overly concerned with who did what, or did not do it. My job was to help get those men out, not point the finger of blame or dish out punishment. I have done that plenty of times in my career. In this case, I am happy to leave that to others.

Instead, I am choosing to focus on all the positive things coming out of that rescue.

In a world so poisoned by the people's evil deeds virtually every single day, I found a great respite up there. Even in the midst of a precarious life-and-death rescue mission. Despite the high stakes, despite the anxiety and concern, there was also a great deal of peace. This peace was born from a shared understanding and a deep respect and gratitude.

It was evident in the local families who would offer me gifts of flowers from their gardens each day to thank me for playing a role in reaching their men, and so I could make an offering at the shrine. It was clear in how our meetings ran, without shouting or anger, but respectfully and collaboratively. It was in the army guys giving me one of their snowsuits to keep me warm. It was inside the mountain, even though it was clearly angry, in the form of those forty-one men being kept warm by the planet's core.

And it was on the faces of countless experts, those at the top of their fields, racing to the source of danger to offer their help in freeing those who were trapped. So many collective deeds of good. So many examples of kindness and selflessness. It was an epic battle of mortals versus a mountain and the gods, it seemed. But everyone was up for the fight.

I am a proud nerd. There is no denying that I am one. I wear nerdy clothing, I talk about nerdy topics, I have a house full of nerdy books and do nerdy pet projects. But together with a bunch of other equally nerdy people, I get to do some pretty incredible stuff.

I think the world could stand to be a nerdier place. It should be one where we celebrate innovation and new ways of thinking, especially around basic stuff that we still do not get right for millions of people. I am talking about clean water, sewage, sanitation and transportation. Why are we happy to condemn so many of our fellow human beings to the horrid realities of not having access to these basic facilities, purely based on where they were born?

We should also embrace other apparently nerdy notions of justice and peace. We should be celebrating the collaboration of good people, the pursuit of positive things, over the manufacture of guns and bombs for the lucrative war and conflict industries.

I have so many misgivings about how modern society has organised itself into a type of intellectual hierarchy. Those who are perceived to be smart get to do the important things. Those who are perceived to be not smart are often denied access. That bothers me. That is not cool.

Everyone should have a seat at the table. The decisions made about the world impact all of us, regardless of the colour of our skin or the skills or qualifications we possess. Everyone has a role to play.

If only we could figure out how to understand each other and appreciate our differences, it would flow through to everything else that matters. If only we could get on the same page about the type of relationship we want with our planet, about what is right and what is wrong, and about how we are all connected.

Far more unites us than divides us. I believe that now more than ever.

Humans are fallible. No-one is perfect. We are all doing our best and we cannot do more than that. We need to have humility and be gentle with each other.

Religion should not be a point of differentiation. It does not need to be this concept that divides us into camps and pits us against each other. It can – and should – be a convergence of thoughts. We should not be troubled about the specifics of a religion, but trust that its core intentions are noble.

I cannot think of a religion that is intrinsically bad. At the heart of it, each is seeking to make the world a better place.

Sometimes, people who follow religions do horrible things, but I do not think that is linked to the faith itself. Rather, I reckon it is a sign of how a particular philosophy has been corrupted for personal gain. No doubt my words here will offend some because of how I speak about gods. All I ask is: don't act harshly against me. I am just swept up in circumstances not of my making. My intentions are honorable.

Scientists should not be angry at people who are religious. They should not resent those who have faith, or look down on them as stupid or naive. Because scientists are also simply seeking truth. We are all trying to understand the purpose of life and how best to live it.

I believe kindness can save the world. Kindness has always led to good outcomes – always.

It does not mean having to risk your life on the other side of the world to save people trapped in a tunnel. It can be small. It could be as innocuous as letting someone into your lane on the road.

You know the scenario. Someone ahead of you in the next lane has their indicator on. You have two choices. One, you can speed up and keep them out, refusing to relinquish even an inch of your space. Or two, you can choose to back off a bit to let them in.

We should choose kindness. We should leave things better than we find them. We should remember that we share this planet with more than 8 billion other people who, really, are no different from us.

We should lift each other up instead of tearing each other down. We should individually play our part to bring a little joy, a little kindness, to our surroundings. Collectively, those small acts of kindness will combine to leave a lasting mark.

And when wonderful things happen to us and those around us, we should share these stories. Not to boast or brag, but to let everyone know that goodness is still a quality that exists. Sometimes, it feels as though there is not much good in the world. I have seen first-hand that there is.

I have a great time talking about it to anyone who will listen.

After the rescue, the first call I made was to my wife, letting her know I was alive. We spoke about the incredible outcome and how relieved and happy I was. She asked me to come home as soon as possible. I agreed; I would be back with her and Trisha soon.

The second call I made was to Trisha's school in Monbulk, asking if I could come to give the kids a presentation when I got back before they went on summer holidays.

I love talking to children about the stuff I do. It fires their brains and excites them. We adults, for the most part, are pretty set in our ways. We are busy doing what we need to do – work, home, sleep. By a certain age, how we view the world is entrenched.

But kids are full of wonder and look at life and everything it involves as being full of endless possibilities. It is easy to inspire them to dream big and reach for the stars. I love that.

I was so energised by the power of good people doing good things that I wanted to share this potent and moving experience with a group of teenagers at my daughter's school. After all, I am conscious of how depressing and hopeless the world can feel to young people these days.

I was keen to show them that it is not all bad out there. There are still good people, working together, who achieve great things. Even if it sometimes does not seem like it, there are.

I also wanted to explain to them that they do not all have to be doctors and lawyers. If they want to work a trade, that is fine. If you want to pursue something creative, that is OK, too.

During the rescue, it was more than OK – it was essential. It was not at all just about engineers and scientists, we needed people to cook the food, do the welding, drive the trucks . . .

Everyone – from all walks of life and backgrounds – was working together to save those forty-one men. We were links in a strong chain. Without one link, the whole thing would have fallen apart. We were all equal. No-one was above anyone else.

The kids really liked that message.

Amid the hundreds of messages cluttering my phone when I was safely back in Melbourne, one stood out – a request from an Indian artist called Murali Surya, who wanted to paint my portrait. On an instinct, I called him back. And in less than 48 hours, there I was, in his studio at dawn, about to be immortalised on canvas.

Murali wanted to paint me nude. Overnight, I had wrestled with the idea. Why not? After all, I'm very much alive, and he's the artist. That morning, I stood before him and shed my clothes.

His reaction was priceless. Shocked by the starkness of my skin, he quickly changed course. It would now be a clothed portrait!

To my surprise, Murali turned out to be an engineer and devout Hindu. This duality in his identity intrigued me. After some reflection, he chose to portray me in a distinctly classical manner – Australian shorts and a humble T-shirt, framed by the symbols of my life's work: my emergency helmet, steel-capped boots, welding face shield, prayer shawl and wedding ring.

As his brush moved across the canvas, we discussed India's nuclear ambitions; Murali's pivotal role in creating the country's first particle accelerator; and the philosophical questions of science, spirituality and love. His wife Rajashree, hailing from Pune, would join us for discussions too. It felt like we weren't just creating a portrait, we were exploring the universe, from physics to the metaphysical.

In his eyes, painting me was part of his destiny. Who am I to argue with that? His painting is more than I could have ever imagined, though I'm yet to find a space bold enough to hang it. It was entered in the 2024 Archibald Prize but didn't make the final exhibition.

Ah, well. Art, like life, is full of surprises.

One feature of this experience is that, for the first time in my life, the job has not ended. Usually, there is a pack-up of some kind. There is a conclusion to things and everyone goes home.

I submit a report, get on a plane and never talk about it again. That is how it tends to go. And yet here I am, a long time since the rescue, still talking about it regularly.

But I am happy with that. A lot of important life lessons can be gleaned from what we achieved up there. The rescue and its successful outcome offer a reminder about the fragility of life and the importance of making the most of what time we have here as mortals.

For me, personally, the rescue has reaffirmed my focus on the greater good. Not on making money, collecting accolades and being the best in my field, but on having an impact on ordinary, everyday people. Even if the impact is abstract. Even if they do not know it.

I feel the most content I have been in my life. In some way, I feel like I discharged the greatest duty of my life. I feel like this was perhaps what I was born to do. It was why I was put on this Earth. No, let me rephrase the point – I feel contentment.

I was part of something bigger than any one person. I was a member of a team.

As content as I am, this lifestyle does take a toll. The physical demands I have put on my body over the years of living this type of intensive travel have been extreme.

One day, I suspect, my flame will go out. And probably not a slow and gentle waning of a candle at the end of its wick, but more of an abrupt snuffing.

Recently, a request came in for a short but packed trip to Europe. Ordinarily, not that long ago, I would have jumped at the chance without much thought. Sure! Why not? That has been my approach to most things these past two decades.

But this time? When Gail flagged the invitation, my immediate response was wildly out of character.

'Ah, shit. Can we just pretend I'm sick?'

I'm not good at saying 'no', though. I never have been. But the older I get, the easier it feels like it could be to offer an answer other than 'yes'.

Each time I fly back home to Australia after spending a few days, weeks or, in some cases, several months in some far-flung country, I am sure it will the last. No-one can have this many adventures in a single lifetime, surely.

I should write some of these stories down, I tell myself. *Surely, nothing this wild will ever happen again.*

Somehow, it hasn't been long until the phone has rung again and I am off once more. Here we go again.

Yesterday, I was planting new pea and bean saplings in the back garden. It was a peaceful and meditative task. No helicopters, no diplomatic escorts, certainly no assassins in the shadows waiting to pounce.

But it felt nice. It was a slow pace that I have never felt comfortable operating at, even for short periods of time, and yet I enjoyed it.

The quiet. The predictability. The momentary solitude.

I could be happy doing this, I thought to myself.

Then the phone rang with an intriguing query. How would I feel about heading to China tomorrow?

ACKNOWLEDGEMENTS

To my mother, Norma – your unwavering belief in the transformative power of education has been a lighthouse guiding me through the stormiest seas. Your constant encouragement shaped my path when doubt and distraction loomed large. And to my beloved wife, Divina – your love is the unshakable foundation on which I stand. Without your support, none of this would have been possible. You two have anchored me in life's most unpredictable tides.

The success of this mission, against all odds, was no solo act. It was a symphony of minds, hands and hearts, all coming together in those perilous mountains.

The steadfast leadership of Prime Minister Narendra Modi, Lieutenant General Hasnain, Uttarakhand Chief Minister Pushkar Singh Dhami, Union Minister V.K. Singh, and Bhaskar Khulbe of the Prime Minister's Office set the tone. But make no mistake: this operation thrived on the relentless grit of the hundreds who worked tirelessly – the welders down in the pits, the hand miners scraping the earth with their bare hands in those final, tense hours. Every single one of you was a vital cog in this extraordinary, intricate machine.

To the cooks, the cleaners, the engineers, the drivers – those who dug an emergency road by hand, pick by pick, shovel by shovel – each and every one of you was essential. To the teams working 24/7 on the auger – the fabricators and operators – bravo. To the vertical drillers who voluntarily halted their work prior to the crucial moment of horizontal breakthrough, your grace in the heat of the moment spoke volumes. Together, we created something that was impossible to achieve alone.

I am especially grateful to those who walked closest with me on this journey – Chris Cooper, Colonel Parikshit Hasan and our elite team of technical specialists. The National Disaster Response Force, the State Disaster Response Force, Inspector Jagdamba Iprasad Bijalwan and the Uttarakhand Police, engineers from the Indian Army Corps of Engineers, Coal India, Geological Survey of India, and Project Shivalik from the Border Roads Organisation – all of you, alongside volunteers and experts from across the globe, made this a truly international effort. If even one of you had been absent, the outcome could have been devastatingly different.

We must also acknowledge our engineers from around the world – even from nations sometimes considered adversaries. In times like these, we – technicians, workers, the doers – transcend borders and politics. Our loyalty lies with the shared mission of improving life for all.

To the companies who lent us your equipment and expertise, you know who you are. From tunnel boring machines to jumbos, the very labels on your products tell the story of your invaluable contributions. I've thanked you all by name on LinkedIn, but here, let me just say this – thank you, truly.

My deepest gratitude goes to the International Tunnelling and Underground Space Association. You stood by me in my role as President, even when my attention was divided by the urgency of this rescue. Missing the ITA 2023 awards wasn't something I planned, but I had forty-one very good reasons. This was a calling I had to answer, and I regret nothing.

To my family – Divina, Sam, Hannah, Edward, Trisha, Mum, Helena, Mark and my newest Indian daughter, Tanzila – thank you for letting me go, knowing that I might not return. Your support empowers me in ways words cannot express. And to my late brother Colin – I hope you were having a puff with Shiva and putting in a good word for me with Kali.

Phil Luke, Steve Gunther, and Simon & Schuster – you pushed me to share this story, and believe me, turning mountains of my typed prose, handwritten notes, video logs and voice memos into a cohesive book was a challenge like no other. I can write a killer legal brief or scientific paper, but a book? That's a whole different game. To Emma Nolan, Rosie McDonald, Jade Gould, and the rest of the publishing team – thank you for making this possible. A special shout-out to Shannon Molloy for helping me find my voice as a storyteller.

A heartfelt thanks to Australia's Prime Minister Anthony Albanese and Opposition Leader Peter Dutton. The fact that you both agreed on something related to me? Now that's a miracle! Are you both OK?

To my teachers across so many disciplines – mathematics, chemistry, physics, geology, law – you've played pivotal roles in shaping who I am today. Special thanks to Colin, my welding instructor; Peter, my truck-driving teacher; Wendy Bourke, the hairdressing queen; Dave Roland, the hunter; Chris, the farmer; Laurence, the builder; and Bob, the submariner – your lessons have been invaluable.

And Gail – you've been there through thick and thin. You understand me better than anyone, and for that, I am eternally grateful.

To my spiritual guides, Manish Kr Meena, Murali the painter, and Shan from the Sri Vakrathunda Vinayagar Temple at the Basin – your wisdom has helped me understand not just the life-and-death challenges we faced in those mountains but the challenges of my entire life.

George Madden – your example of decency and integrity in your roles as lawyer, husband and father have inspired me deeply. In our next lives, let's be bound by blood.

Monbulk's Maggie, Yvonne, and Becky – thank you for the warmest homecoming I could have ever hoped for. Your joy is infectious. To the community of Monbulk, your sanctuary has been my home for thirty years, from scones and cream at the police station to barefoot bowls and the farmer's market. And yes, I must mention the excitement over the reopening of the fish and chip shop in October 2024 – Monbulk, I love you.

To Norma Van Eck – you've been Mum's best friend for what seems like a thousand years. Pete and Val – here's a shoutout to Cohuna! And let's not forget my utterly spectacular failure as a beekeeper.

Lastly, Rahul Gupta – the man behind the curtain. Your calm, technical brilliance orchestrated this operation like a maestro leading a symphony. More than a colleague, you are my brother. You knew the risks, and you told me to stay out of that tunnel, but I'm glad I didn't listen.

History reminds us that miracles are real, as recorded in the ancient epics – *The Iliad*, *The Epic of Gilgamesh*, *The Aeneid*, *Shahnameh*, *Beowulf*. There is something eternal about the battle between mortals, gods and mountains. And that's exactly what happened here.

In November 2023, during Diwali, a seventeen-day battle raged between a group of brave individuals, a mountain and the gods. Incredibly, all forty-one trapped souls and every single rescuer walked away unharmed, safe and reunited with their families. Not a single drop of blood was shed.

On any view, this was nothing short of a miracle.

For the first time in more than sixty years, I can finally say with certainty – I am content.

ABOUT THE AUTHOR

Arnold Dix is an Australian geologist, engineer, barrister, farmer and truck driver, who is widely known for being a tunnelling expert. In November 2023 he played a crucial role in the seventeen-day rescue operation to save forty-one miners trapped in the Uttarkashi tunnel in India. All workers were freed successfully. He was also involved in the 9/11 disaster in New York, the London Bombings, the Madrid Bombings and in a program in Qatar helping to improve conditions for the enslaved workers who were building facilities for the World Cup.

Scan here for links to Arnold's photos, videos and Spotify playlist